◇◇◇

Acting on the Script

Bruce Miller

APPLAUSE
THEATRE & CINEMA BOOKS
An Imprint of
Hal Leonard Corporation

Published in 2014 by Applause Theatre & Cinema Books
An Imprint of Hal Leonard Corporation
7777 West Bluemound Road
Milwaukee, WI 53213

Trade Book Division Editorial Offices
33 Plymouth St., Montclair, NJ 07042

Ten-Dollar Drinks reprinted courtesy of Joe Pintauro

Toward the Sun, by Alan Haehnel and Bruce Miller. Copyright © 2013 by Alan Haehnel and Bruce Miller. To purchase acting editions of *Toward the Sun*, or to obtain stock and amateur performance rights, please contact Playscripts, Inc. www.playscripts.com (info@playscripts.com / 1-866-NEW-PLAY [639-7529]).

Printed in the United States of America

Book design by Lynn Bergesen

Library of Congress Cataloging-in-Publication Data

Miller, Bruce J.
  Acting on the script / Bruce Miller.
     pages cm
  ISBN 978-0-87910-825-0 (pbk.)
  1. Drama—Explication. 2. Acting. I. Title.
  PN1707.M535 2014
  808.2'3—dc23
                                          2014012035

www.applausebooks.com

To all my students,
whom I have tried to inspire.

And to my daughter, Emma,
who continues to inspire me.

CONTENTS

Contents

PREFACE

Since you are reading the words on this page, it is no great leap of logic to assume that you are an actor, or are trying to becoming one. And with an even smaller leap I might assume that you picked up this book because you are looking for answers—for some meaningful "how to's" that will help you become the best actor you can be. So let me ask you a question right at the outset. What do you think it takes to become a first-rate actor? Take a moment to think about it. You may even want to jot your thoughts down. Doing so makes them more tangible and, in my opinion, more useful. In the course of reading this book you will be asked to do a lot of thinking. And one of the goals of this book is to make your thinking as useful as possible for you as an actor. Thinking is really what this book is all about—learning to think as an actor must. So—when you're finished thinking, continue reading.

Talent may have been the first answer that came to mind, particularly if you're just beginning your acting training. But talent can't be learned; you either have it or you don't. Talent is a gift—so if you've got it, say thank you and read on. Now, on the other hand, if you said *craft*, you identified something that can be learned and will help you use your talent more effectively. In addition to being an art form, acting is very much a craft, because it calls for skills that can be learned and mastered. Many if not most artists in the field have studied acting as a craft, even if they haven't done so formally. And if you think you don't have talent, or don't have as much as you'd like, craft will help you appear as if you do.

So let's refine our question: What are the skills that can be learned and mastered that can make you a good actor? If you're familiar with Stanislavski, you may want to say finding emotional truth, or sense memory, or playing actions. If you're familiar with the Method, you may say personal investment or emotional accessibility. Those of you familiar with the work of Sanford Meisner may say the ability to listen and react truthfully in the moment. Those of you familiar with Grotowski, Laban, or Michael Chekhov may say being able to access and use your body effectively. Others still might reference the vocal work of Linklater, Fitzmaurice, or Cicely Berry. Still others might say it's all about relaxation. And if you've already had some training, you probably know that acting requires that you be skilled in all these areas. And that is why universities, conservatories, and acting studios everywhere feature workshops, courses, and, on the graduate level, even degrees in all these areas. And ultimately you will want to develop as many of these skills as you possibly can.

But there is another area of study you will need to be skilled in as well, and it is as important that you master this subject as any of the other skills listed—perhaps even more so. And yet it is a subject that you will find listed very sparely on curriculum menus. I certainly never had a course in it in graduate school, and most undergraduate programs offer it as a general course serving all theatre majors no matter what their particular focus. In the program where I teach, for instance, it has only been added as a separate course for BFA actors very recently. (Actually, I have been teaching the course for years, but we have finally begun calling it what it is.) What I'm talking about is *script analysis and synthesis* for actors. And we finally gave it its own title because, as one of the most important skills to be mastered, it deserves one.

Don't get me wrong. Many programs offer a course or two in script analysis. But the way a lighting or set designer must learn to take apart a play and put it back together is different from what an actor must learn to do. And though writing and directing share some analytical requirements with acting, only actors are fully responsible for making the whole story work at every moment they are on stage. A general course in play analysis cannot give you all the skills you need to carry this enormous responsibility. Nor will it give you adequate time and opportunity to develop those skills so you can make them a part of your actor's tool kit and be able to use them reliably and independently.

As a result, for many if not most actors, learning to analyze and synthesize a play becomes a byproduct of our preparation in scene study classes or part of our on-the-job training. Script analysis remains a supporting player, when it should have a leading role in the training process. This is a disturbingly wrong-headed treatment of one of our most important tools, and it leaves the actor in a similar position to that of the young college student forced to learn to read and write up to level after years of sneaking by in his or her primary education. An inability to understand and use a script effectively can turn acting into a hit-or-miss affair, where choices come out of trial and error rather than through a dependable application of craft.

Our primary job as actors is to tell the story of a play clearly, compellingly, and believably. In order to do that, we have to know what the story is and how to present it effectively. We have to know what the best choices are and how to make them. This is a skill that must be developed systematically, through practice and repetition. It must be a focus of attention, not the byproduct of other work. It is the foundation of all that we do when we work from a script. So why is it not taught with the same commitment as voice work or movement?

I can't tell you how often I have seen even professional actors in class or auditions present work that makes no sense in the context of

the play—choices that are simply not based on what the script is telling them they must show or do. On stage, those choices obscure the
meaning of the play—and the actors come across as deficient along
with the story. Unfortunately, they hardly ever realize that this is
what is keeping them and their work from fully succeeding.

This book, like its partner, *Actor's Alchemy*, will examine the relationship between the script and what an actor ultimately does on the
stage or on screen. It is my belief that when actors learn to use their
scripts with the appropriate analytical insights, they are better able to
find and execute choices that will make the story they are telling clear
and compelling, and make the work they do more believable as well.
As you will see in the pages that follow, I am as concerned with the
doing and *feeling* aspects of acting as the next acting teacher, but it is
my belief that all your doings and feelings must be connected to what
the playwright has set out. Therefore, the ability to analyze a script
and make it the source for all the work you put on stage should be an
essential part of your process.

In the chapters that follow, you will learn how to use a script in
a logical, effective, and commonsense way. First you'll discover an
approach to the script that will serve you as an actor. Then you'll
begin to apply your new analytical tools in a short play. Finally, you'll
be able to strengthen those skills with a series of etudes (practice
scenes) to work through in a scene study class. By the end of the book,
you will have a process for reading and understanding a script as an
actor must, and the skill set to determine the choices you must make
if you are going to efficiently serve the material, your production,
and the character you are playing. Included within these pages you
will find:

- A review of the basic tools of acting craft and how they are
  interconnected with analysis and synthesis

- An overview of your responsibility as a storyteller to make effective choices based on script work
- A set of guidelines for making effective choices
- A road map for making choices based on conflict and objective playing
- A process for finding the clues in a script
- A process for finding character through analysis and subsequent choices
- A system for effective scoring of a scene
- A complete analysis and scoring of a play by Joe Pintauro
- Eight original scenes written especially to help you become proficient at analysis and synthesis
- Useful commentary on all scenes to guide you through the process of analysis and synthesis
- Context to help you connect your analysis and synthesis choices to the other aspects of acting necessary for successful work

The repetition you will encounter as you progress through the book is intentional. When you have read and worked to the end, you may wish to consult individual chapters, and the quick refreshers you find there will help to ground you in the process as you focus on particular points or challenges. What is more, you are aiming for mastery—for the point where you no longer have to think about your process—and mastery requires plenty of practice and repetition. By exposing you to basic principles again and again, I hope to etch them into your memory so that they will be there when you need them.

Acting on
the Script

PART ONE

Analysis

⟨⟨⟨⟨⟨⟨⟨⟨⟨⟨⟨⟨⟨⟨⟨⟨⟨⟨⟨⟨⟨⟨⟨⟨⟨⟨⟨⟨⟨⟨⟨⟨⟨⟨⟨⟨⟨⟨

Introduction to Part One

Every year my freshman BFA actors spend their first semester of training learning how to behave believably on stage. They learn to relax their bodies, to move and gesture and do business. They learn to re-create their real-life behavior by doing Hagen work. They learn to conduct themselves on stage as human beings do in life. They learn to listen and react from moment to moment through Meisner work and improv. And all is well—until I put scripts in their hands and tell them to act.

Suddenly, all the believability they worked so hard on goes down the drain. Suddenly, what they say and do makes little sense at all. Why? Mostly because the choices they make or fail to make have no connection to the script and story they are working with. The lines they deliver don't sound believable because they don't make sense in the context of the story they are supposedly telling. They move awkwardly or not at all, unsure of what to do with their bodies because the script seems to be working against them. In other words, they try to act before they understand the script they are supposedly bringing to life.

As an actor, your work should always start with the story. Before you do anything else, you must learn to find the story contained in the script. It is essential that you learn to think that way. Story first; always story first. And the story the playwright has set down is told through a combination of what the characters say and what the characters do. Sometimes the playwright literally tells you in the script what the characters are doing through the dialogue and through stage direction. But sometimes the characters' actions are implied, not by explicit instructions in the script, but by the story the playwright is telling.

Too often, beginning actors use only the dialogue to figure out the story, and much of the time that leaves them lost and confused. Playwrights tell their stories through the combination of what their characters say and do. The dialogue is only a tool, no more or less important than the physical actions those characters execute and the psychological actions they play out through the course of the play. And it is the action combined with the dialogue that makes the story clear and compelling. Ultimately, as an actor, you must be able to step back and imagine the script performed as an audience might see it and hear it. The audience takes in the play with their eyes and ears, discovering the story both through the dialogue and through what they see the characters do.

That is why you must never take dialogue at face value. A literal interpretation of dialogue will usually lead you nowhere. Skilled actors realize that any dialogue must be taken in its greater context only. So you must learn to read a script in that way. Let me explain. If I say to you, "I love you," for instance, it doesn't literally mean I love you. You will automatically understand the phrase in terms of its contextual meaning. Maybe I said "I love you" because you said something insightful or funny. Maybe I said it because you said or did something hurtful and I was using sarcasm to mask my wound. The point is, you would know because of our relationship and the context the comment was said in. You would know that I was not literally proclaiming my love.

4

As actors deciphering a script you will need to look at the context and given circumstances in which the dialogue is spoken. Remember, the story drives how the dialogue will be delivered, not the other way around. The story drives the action and creates the conflict from which you will determine your objectives and tactics. Doing this analysis will inform your decisions about how you speak your lines on stage. If you take the dialogue at face value, you will seldom sound believable or make sense of the story the playwright has provided.

All playwrights know that if a story is to work effectively, it must be planned out meticulously. If the playwright knows his craft, then that is exactly what he will do. A well-put-together story, like a fine watch, has a set of gears that work together in total synchronicity. All the elements in a good story are necessary and work effectively together. It is your job to translate what's on the page to what is on the stage clearly and effectively, and to add to the playwright's vision of the story. Once the job has been turned over to you, it's in your hands to be the best storyteller you can possibly be. And clear and effective storytelling is no easy task.

If you're not a good joke teller, you know just what I mean. You've probably found yourself leaving out a vital plot point that you've had to go back and fill in, or you've gotten to the end of the joke and realized that you failed to set it up properly. You can't go back, so you bravely deliver the punch line to no response. And once again you swear you'll never tell another joke in your life. Delivering the story of the play is not quite as difficult, because you've got the lines memorized and the physical story well rehearsed. But you've got to find the story before you can tell it. Then, once you find it, as a storyteller you need to know how to build the tension and keep the audience asking, "What will happen next?"

You may be thinking at this point, "I thought that was the director's job," and sometimes the director does take on this responsibility. But this book is intended to make you director proof. That means you will know what to do whether or not the director addresses your acting choices. So, in order to do your job effectively as an actor, you must know the storytelling gears and understand how they work together effectively. That's what the first part of this book is all about.

◇◇◇

CHAPTER ONE

The Tools of the Craft

It's always amazing to watch my students when they are doing acting exercises or improv work. The spontaneity, creativity, and listening skills they demonstrate are often breathtaking. At these times I often find myself fantasizing about all the future Meryl Streeps, Kate Winslets, and Daniel Day-Lewises I will have taught. Invariably, though, when the ten-ton boulder we call the script is passed amongst my students, these fantasies vanish into the ether. In that moment, genius disappears, replaced by an actorish bunch that seem to have not a clue as to why they are uttering the words flowing from their mouths. Worse, these creatures, unlike the gifted artists that preceded them, can't seem to listen to each other even for an instant, so busy are they attempting to demonstrate their skill at reading, or performing simulated acts of human behavior.

Maybe this description sounds familiar to you. It is the reason that over the years I have come to rely far less on exercises and acting games in the classroom, and far more on the study of scripted work. The exercises and games just don't seem to translate reliably into the development of dependable acting skills. Scene study work has a far better track record.

Obviously, I'm not the only one who has noticed this phenomenon. Universally, the scene study class is the most common format for the all-around teaching of acting skills and for brushing them up. In New York, L.A., and Chicago, scores of scene study classes are offered at any given time. This is the case in most university theatre departments as well. Once the intro class in acting is out of the way, most students find themselves pursuing the study of acting in a scene study format. Whether it's Shakespeare, Chekhov, or contemporary American drama, the scene study class seems to provide the best venue for applying and mastering the basic skills necessary for success—success being here defined as an actor who can get work, and knows how to work independently once hired.

So, what exactly are these skills that you must have if you are going to be employable? Here is a list of some of the essentials.

- You must be able to analyze a script.
- You must be able to make appropriate choices based on your analysis of that script—choices that tell the story of the play, the scene, and your character clearly and effectively. All of these choices must make sense for the character and serve to illuminate and advance the story.
- You must be able to move, behave, and talk like an actual human being, even when you are working from the script.
- You must be able to listen and react from moment to moment in a seemingly spontaneous way.
- You must produce work that is interesting at a minimum, but far better if it is compelling.

Scene study is an effective way to develop all of those essential acting skills, because it is a process of taking apart the script and then making choices based on what you have learned. We call this analysis and synthesis, and it is the focus of this book. But scene study is not the first step in the process. It is assumed that the students who register for a scene study class have had some prior acting training. It is also assumed that these students are familiar with the basics of acting craft and know how to use them. On the college level, students are required to have an intro class before setting foot in a scene study studio. I have on occasion taught students outside of the academic arena who want to be actors and jump into scene study without having had any previous training. When they have good instincts and some natural talent, many of them have been able to pick up the vocabulary and basic tools of the craft as they go. But obviously this approach is far more difficult than coming into scene study with a basic understanding of process and the necessary skills.

I, by the way, was one of those students who was thrust into a scene study class without prior training, and it meant a lot of playing catch-up and lots of running blind. The tension thus created kept me from being fully available in the moment (an essential part of good acting) or comfortably relaxed while working (another necessity for professional actors). I also developed bad habits because there were basic craft concepts that I never really absorbed or correctly understood. So it does make sense that you spend an appropriate amount of time learning the basics of acting craft before stepping into the scene study arena.

Here is a list of craft terms that you should be familiar with and have a handle on before venturing into scene study. There are many more, but for our purposes, let's start with these. See how many of the terms listed below you are familiar with and know how to use. Then think about how many of these concepts you actually make part of your to-do list when you are preparing your own work.

Story   Justifying the action
Arc or throughline   Stakes, risk, and urgency
Action   Given circumstances
Conflict   Character
Obstacles   Physical action
Objectives   "As if's"
Tactics   The "magic if"
Beats   Listening and reacting
Transitions   Emotion
Victories, defeats, discoveries

Now let's review the meaning of these terms and how these tools of the craft actually work for us as actors.

Telling the Story

Every play or film script tells a story—hopefully a good one. All stories consist of character, dialogue, and action. If the playwright is good, everything she has put into the script is there for a reason. Everything in it has purpose. The action happens in a particular time and place for a reason, and the good story usually has something of value to say. An actor must know what that story is and how it works before he can begin to tell it. As an actor you must be able to recognize the story elements that the playwright has given you, and know your character's responsibility for telling that story effectively. The good actor will discover the reason why every element of the script is there and find ways to use those ingredients effectively.

Arc

All stories have a beginning, middle, and end. The story starts somewhere and ends somewhere else. The bigger the distance from the beginning to end, the more interesting the journey. Characters in a play also have an arc. The most interesting characters are changed by what happens during the course of the play. The bigger the change, the more interesting the character. The skilled actor will chart these changes through the script and know how to make clear when and how they occur during the journey. The audience will see these changes only through what the actor as character chooses to do and how he does it.

Action

This term has several meanings for an actor. It can refer to the cause-and-effect events of a play—how one thing leads to another in terms of plot. This use is interchangeable with *arc* or *throughline* as defined above. Action can also refer to the psychological and physical actions the actor as character chooses to engage in. Psychological action refers to the goals that a character is pursuing at all times (see *objective* below), and physical action refers to the things a character actually does physically, moment by moment, during the course of the play or script. These two kinds of action are usually connected in that both share the same purpose: to satisfy a particular need or achieve a particular goal. It is important to keep in mind that action, no matter which kind, is a central ingredient of all drama and is always closely connected to conflict.

Conflict and Obstacles

Every good story starts with conflict. It is often referred to as the engine of drama. Though there are three basic kinds of conflict—person versus person, person versus him- or herself, and person against some outside force like nature or society—the most common conflicts that actors work with are person versus person and person versus him- or herself (internal conflict). The vast majority of scenes that playwrights invent consist of two people with a conflict between them. Each of those characters wants or needs something from the other or is trying to keep the other from doing something.

There are situations, however, when a conflict is not so obvious—in a love scene, for instance. In those situations, the playwright has probably invented something that keeps a character from pursuing the love that he or she wants. That thing that stands in the way may something internal—a fear or belief, perhaps, that prevents the character from pursuing the thing he or she most desires. How many times in the *Wizard of Oz* is Dorothy slowed down by doubt in herself? Those doubts are her internal *obstacles*—goal blockers that serve to keep the conflict intense even when the characters don't seem to be at odds. The thing that keeps a character from his or her goal can be external as well. Dorothy needs to get to the Emerald City to see the Wizard, but she faces many obstacles that she must overcome while traveling on the Yellow Brick Road. She must elude magic spells, escape from kidnappers, and more before she can return to her primary objective: to find a way home.

Objectives and Tactics

While human beings do not always know why they do and say the things they do, actors playing characters must always know. Whether or not the *characters they are playing* know the reasons for their own actions is a different question and an important distinction. Unlike in life, where things often happen randomly, there is nothing random about a script. As noted earlier, the playwright has carefully planned out all that happens. Though a play or film may seem just like life when well written and acted, it is not—because everything has been predetermined by the writer. The events of a play are like a set of railroad tracks on which the train that rides them has no choice but to follow. The actor playing a character knows this and must make and execute choices accordingly.

Remember, the playwright has written her story based on some kind of conflict between the characters. It is your job as the actor to determine the conflict and find out how your character contributes to that conflict. In other words, you need to figure out what it is you want or need from the other character you are acting with. The other character's needs, in opposition to yours, should provide the necessary ingredients that make up a strong conflict. The need that you aim to satisfy is your *objective, intention, action*, or *goal*. You will pursue this objective at all times. That is worth repeating. You will play your objective at all times.

Imagine how much more effective we would be in life if, during our every waking moment, we single-mindedly pursued our every want and need! Our lives would be dramatic and intense and unrelenting. That's what you want from a script, and that's what the good playwright has given you—if you know how to read that map we call the script, and if you know how to effectively build choices from that script.

Once you have figured out your objective, you will have to figure out how your character will achieve it. With practice, you will learn to recognize how much the playwright has provided. By using the dialogue and action in that moment, you will find *tactics* that get you toward what you as the character need. When your tactics are working, you will continue to use them; if they don't work or stop working, then you will give up those tactics and try something else. Sometimes you will know when to give up a tactic or objective simply by looking at the script. It will be clear in the writing. At other times, you will discover when to change your strategy as you rehearse your work from moment to moment.

Beats, Transitions, Victories, Defeats, and Discoveries

In acting terms, a beat is the length of script during which a character pursues a particular objective or tactic. The actor playing the character will continue to pursue an objective or tactic until he gets what he needs (a victory), fails to get what he needs (a defeat), or decides to stop pursuing that goal for a particular reason. He may discover new information that causes a change of objective or tactic, or something more important or immediate may interrupt the action of the moment. Here are some examples that should help clarify all this.

Suppose your character is a police officer trying to talk a man down from a very high window ledge. You are standing on the balcony beside the window where the man is lodged. The script calls for you to talk about his bright future, about the family that will miss him, about the shame he is currently feeling. You even offer him tickets to a World Series game if he will step down. You crack a few jokes; you try to make him talk to his wife on the phone. All of these things are the tactics you use in pursuing your objective to get the man off the ledge. All of these tactics are in the script. They are part of the dialogue. But how you will say them is for you to discover.

In telling the story of this scene, it is your job to recognize the victories, defeats, and discoveries in the script. And whenever there is a victory or defeat, or new information that changes things, you must define that moment through your acting choices and follow it with a transition—a change from one objective or tactic to another.

Justifying the Action

As just noted, many transitional moments are built into the script. In the situation mentioned above, the change of subject from the man's bright future to the family that will miss him is just such an example. But why does the police officer initiate that transition? It will be your job to find the reason and make it clear by your acting choices. You must *justify* all the action stated in the play or implied by the play. The script dictates that you change subjects, but does not necessarily tell you why or how. It is your responsibility to figure that out and to make acting choices that make the reason clear and believable.

Suppose that while you are talking about his future, the man on the ledge takes a step toward the abyss. You see that you have agitated the man, so you switch to the subject of his family. You have just made sense of the dialogue rather than simply stating the lines. That is justification. You note that the new tactic calms the man down, so you keep talking about his wife and children until you see that it is no longer having a calming effect. There is another transition. You change tactics again. All of this must be shown through the actions you and your acting partner come up with.

Now suppose that the written dialogue suggests that the man gets more and more agitated despite what you say and do. You sense that he is about to jump, so you give up your tactic and take on a new objective. You grab at him from your balcony position. You pull him in. That's a victory. You must play it. You miss and he jumps. That is a defeat. You must play it. A transition always follows, and you must then find a new objective to play.

All right, how about this one—just as the man is about to jump, a new character enters the scene. It is the man's daughter. He sees her and suddenly becomes calm. An interruption and new information change the course of the scene, and new objectives will be formed as a result. For any change of objective or tactic, a transition occurs. Sometimes these transitions are major events and take time. In other situations, they are almost instantaneous. But, following any transition, the actor as character must find a new objective to play. And all actions—whether stated or implied in the script, or added in by the actors as characters—must be justified. Everything must make sense and add to the ongoing story.

You must always justify what is in the script, stated or implied. On the other hand, you may never do things as your character that the script cannot support. In other words, if you are the cop and you choose to grab the man as he is about to jump, that is a strong and interesting choice. But you can't do that if it is inconsistent with what the script gives you. If in the script the man jumps, then he must jump. Your choices must be justified by the script in the same way that it is your job to justify what is actually in the script. Your good storytelling must be consistent with the railroad tracks set down by the playwright.

Stakes, Risk, and Urgency

In the list of things that make you employable, you read that the successful actor must be interesting if not compelling. In other words, being believable as an actor isn't always enough; you must also be exciting to watch. You can ensure that this will be the case if you always consider the *stakes* at hand, take *risks* whenever and wherever possible, and make sure that you play with as much *urgency* as the situation allows.

In the scenario regarding the man on the ledge, the playwright has created a situation that is literally life and death. The stakes are the highest possible. A man's life is on the line. In some ways that makes it easy for you as an actor. You won't have to concern yourself so much with being compelling. Just make sure your choices and execution are believable. You will want to make choices that maximize the built-in urgency of the situation. Making choices that are blasé or that work against the excitement that the situation naturally provides would be counterproductive to telling the most exciting story possible. So never do that. Play the highest stakes you possibly can—at all times.

But not all situations are life and death. Sometimes the subject matter of a script or scene reflects ordinary, everyday life. What then? Just be boring? Do boring things? Not at all. Never choose to be boring. The fact is that actors are storytellers as much as playwrights are. It is your job to tell the best story you can—at every moment. Never choose to minimize an acting situation. You must find the urgency in every moment, even when it is not apparent.

How might this work? In the scene you're playing, you and a friend are looking on the Internet for a movie to go see—a common situation. Make it important to you. It's a movie you *really want* to see. Or perhaps in your scene you're looking in the pantry, trying to find a cereal that appeals to you. Find a reason to make it important to you. You're really hungry; you're in need of protein prior to the big game. Here's another. You're cutting your toenails. Make it difficult; make it a challenge. Find a reason and make it important to you. Any situation, even if mundane, can be compelling—if you have the imagination to find the believable high stakes and urgency in it.

Before we leave this subject, notice the subtle differences in meaning of the words *high stakes, urgency,* and *risk.* When the stakes are very high, whatever it is you are doing becomes very important and failure could mean a great loss. Urgency suggests that whatever is at stake must be tended to immediately—right now, or else! When you risk something, it suggests that failure will mean personal loss, so a lot is at stake for you, personally. Think about all the ways this approach could make your work more interesting—better yet, more compelling. And, by the way, get in the habit of considering the specific meaning, not just of words like these that characterize your acting choices, but of every word in your script! All words have specific meanings, and playwrights choose their words very carefully. So be sure to examine those words very closely as an actor.

In summary, then, take risks. Dare to be exciting by doing exciting things, or by doing them in an exciting way. Even when on the face of the script nothing exciting seems to be going on, you can find the excitement in it. That is your job. If you find what you are doing interesting, so will the audience. If that big thing you choose to do can be justified in the script and you can make it believable, go for it. If it's too much, your director or acting teacher will tell you so and you can pull it back. But there is no bigger crime on stage than being boring. The trick with exciting choices is keeping those choices believable. If you can make an audience accept your choices and they can be justified in the script, then it's not too much.

Given Circumstances

Given circumstances define the who, what, when, and where of the play or scene you find yourself in. They can provide the justification for all that you do as a character and how you do it. In addition, understanding and using the who, what, when, and where will help you as an actor to find the urgency in any situation.

Who you are as a character defines how you will do the things that you do. If you as the cop are a shy, retiring kind of person, this information will help you determine how you will say and do what you do. If you're playing the character on the ledge, knowing you are an angry and hostile character will inform how you deal with the cop. Your age as a character will also inform your choices. Your place in society will inform your character. Whether you are religious or secular, rich or poor, educated or ignorant—any and all of this information can be used to develop choices for your character. Anything you come to know about your character can and will help you to make and execute appropriate and interesting choices.

The *what* usually refers to the specifics of the situation you're involved in as well as the backstory. If, for instance, the cop knows that he has terminal cancer, this may allow him to behave differently than he did before his diagnosis. Or suppose the cop has just found out that his wife is divorcing him. That too may influence how he behaves in this situation. Ask yourself how these specifics might affect your behavior if you were playing the cop. Now make up some other specifics and think through how this new information might influence the story and each of the characters' behavior moment by moment.

The *when* refers to anything having to do with time. If the scenario took place in the morning, how would that be different than if it took place at night? Would it be different if it occurred in summer rather than winter? Why and how? If you've been imagining this story in the present day, how would it change if you moved it back in time to 1910? It is your job as an actor to think through these things and adjust your choices accordingly.

How might the *where* affect the story? Would the story be different if it occurred in Minneapolis versus, say, New York? Would the characters be different as well? How? Why? How about if the story happened in Paris, or Seattle? On Mars, or Venus? I'm not trying to be silly. If the playwright sets a play in a particular time and place, there are reasons for it. Your job is to figure out why it happens where it does and when it does, and to make interesting choices based on your investigation. Custom, style, and politics all influence behavior, and are just a few of the considerations that will be affected by time and place.

Character

One of my least favorite things to hear a student say is any phrase that contains the words "being the character." There are some truly gifted actors who claim to "become" their character while working, but most actors are unable to access such an experience with any reliability. Since most actors have to work whether they're *feeling* their character or not, most actors want and need to define their character through that character's actions. You can play your character's actions no matter how you're feeling—and if they are well chosen, those actions will communicate that character to the audience.

When others describe us in real life, that description is based on the things others see us do and the manner in which we do them. It is no different when we are acting. An audience cannot see into our hearts and minds. They do not penetrate our souls. They see us as characters in a series of situations and determine who we are by our actions—by what we say and do and how we say and do it.

That is how the audience will come to know and understand the cop and the would-be jumper in the scenario above as well. In other words, your job is not to play your character directly, nor is it to become the character. Rather, it is about making appropriate choices—both physical and psychological—for the character you are playing. If you can do that specifically and compellingly, the audience will see who you are as a character in the same way the people in your life have determined who you are. If you are among the fortunate few who can magically become your character without working through the kind of choices we have been talking about, more power to you. For the rest of us, however, it's about finding the actions to play and how to play them.

Physical Actions

Physical actions refer to all the things you physically do on stage. These include movement from place to place; business—ongoing activities like reading the paper, doing push-ups, washing the dishes, etc.; and gesture—such as giving someone the bird or the peace sign. The important thing to remember is that an audience learns about you as much through what you do and how you do it as they do through what you say. That means that everything you physically do is important as an actor playing a character—so your physical behavior cannot be left to spontaneity and inspiration alone. Your physicality must be purposeful. If you move toward someone, your movement has a purpose. If you move away, it is for a reason. How you do your push-ups or read the paper tells us about your character. The finger you give your teacher and how you give it tells us about who you are. Spontaneity and inspiration are good, but the things that happen that way are not necessarily all brilliant or useful. It is your job to sift through it all. It is your job to get rid of what doesn't work or work well enough, and to keep and build on what does.

The "Magic If"

The "magic if" is a tool invented by Stanislavski, the father of acting craft, to help an actor make appropriate choices. Essentially, the "magic if" refers to the answer to the question, "What would I do if I were this character in this situation?" Note that the question is not "What would *I* do if *I* were in this situation?" What you would do may be very different from what the character would do. Your job, based on your analysis of the script, the scene, and the given circumstances regarding the who of your character, is to decide what he or she would do.

21

"As If's"

An "as if" is a tool that will allow you to find something specific and honest to do in a moment where personal experience cannot give you a clear frame of reference. You are using an "as if" when you find an analogous situation from your life in order to explore ways to play specific circumstances in a scene. For instance, in the scene you are working on, you have to play the moment you hear that your best friend has been killed in a car accident. This has never happened to you, but you do remember what you felt like and, more importantly, what you did the moment you heard the news of your grandfather's passing. Remembering those details may help you make appropriate and truthful choices in your scene.

Listening and Reacting

Listening and reacting spontaneously at every moment of your stage life is essential. Time and again you will hear the truly fine actors say that great acting is about reacting. Listening in the moment is a crucial, make-or-break skill, but it is one that stands apart from the rest of the work we have been doing in this chapter. Being available to listen in the moment and reacting spontaneously after so much careful planning may seem to be a contradiction, but it is not. How can you do all this analysis, make all these choices, and still listen and react, you may be asking. Here is the answer.

During the homework and rehearsal process you will make choices and try them out. Your focus and attention will be split between what you need to do and what is going on from moment to moment. Eventually, though, you will be so well rehearsed that you won't have to think about the things you need to do any longer. All of that will be in your muscle memory. Your attention will then be totally in the moment, listening to your scene partner with all your senses, just as you would in life. It is then that your acting becomes totally reactive. It is then that the magic will really begin to happen.

Emotion

Beginners and some emotion-based actors like to talk about their acting in terms of what their characters are feeling. Action-based actors talk about what their characters are doing. In case you haven't figured it out by now, the approach to acting you have been reading about in this book is action-based. Actions can be repeated and controlled. You can perform an action even when you're not feeling it, or feeling it as much as you'd like to, or as much as you did the day before. Everyone can learn to execute actions; not everyone can feel the motion, as Morales from *A Chorus Line* once noted. Don't get me wrong; there is an important place for developing your emotional sensitivities as an actor, but action-based acting will serve you even as you continue to study more sophisticated or alternative approaches to your craft. The fact is, when you commit to an action that is appropriate for the moment and consistent with obtaining your objective, emotions will follow. Human beings are wired that way. If you doubt me, try stroking your pillow like it is the cheek of someone you care about. Bet you feel the love. Now try punching the pillow like it is your worst enemy. Feel the anger; feel the hate. Commit to the action; the rest will take care of itself.

So, there's the rundown of the basic tools of craft you should be using before you tackle a scene study class. In the next chapter, we'll add a few more tools to your tool kit and look more specifically at how they can be applied to a script. In the meantime, you may want to begin watching some films and television shows with an eye toward breaking down what you are viewing into actual acting components.

Of course, if you can find some theatre acting to watch, that will be even better. You'll be surprised to find how much craft is actually on display when you know what you're looking for. A caveat, however: don't become so fanatical about analyzing what you watch that you lose the pleasure of being an audience. Do the analysis after you watch the show, or, better yet, set aside some time and do it on a second viewing...and third, and fourth...You'll be amazed at what you can learn.

◇◇◇◇◇◇◇◇◇◇◇◇◇◇◇◇◇◇◇◇◇◇◇◇◇◇◇◇◇◇◇◇◇◇

CHAPTER TWO

Choices Tell the Story

Did it occur to you before reading Chapter One that actors must be good storytellers? Or that your primary function as an actor is to tell the story clearly and effectively? If your answer is "no," you are not alone. I suspect that few beginning actors think about acting in these terms. What's more, I suspect that many experienced actors don't, either. Acting classes seldom focus on the story and how to tell it. For most of us, at least when we begin our acting training, acting is almost exclusively about being believable. Our focus is generally on learning how to say and do things in a way that looks and sounds like real people saying and doing real things. We're not necessarily trained to take on the responsibility of bringing the script to life and working to enhance its story. But the best actors, and certainly the most versatile ones, do spend a lot of time thinking about the story and their place in that story.

I'll go even further than that. If you are planning on being the best actor you can be, you will need to be able to do the following:

- Understand the story you are telling
- Understand the mechanics of that story

- Make choices based on that understanding that will clarify the action of the overall story and of your character
- Understand how the character you are playing fits into that overall story
- Make choices for your character that further that overall story as well as that of your character
- Make choices that clarify the story of your character in terms of who you are and why you do the things you do
- Make choices at every moment that reveal what you are thinking and feeling as a character to the degree that the script demands

What must never be forgotten is your overall storytelling obligation to the playwright and to the audience. That means your character must never be more important than the part of the central story your character is responsible for telling. If your choices for your character do not fall within the regular movement of the perfectly working solar system we call the script, you are not doing your job correctly.

It is not easy to analyze a script in the way an actor must. In your high school and college literature classes, you have spent most of your time learning to analyze short stories, novels, and plays in ways that, unfortunately, do not serve you well as an actor. If you are a good student in your English class and do the work assigned, you probably get ticked at your teacher when the focus turns to plot. Any good student who actually takes the trouble to read *The Scarlet Letter* gets in a huff when the teacher wants to talk about "what happened next." You want to get to the whys and hows. Is the Reverend Dimmesdale really evil; is Hester responsible for what happened to her? What was Hawthorne really saying in his novel, and how does it relate to his short story "Young Goodman Brown"? These are all great questions, and the intelligent, curious student should want to get to the bottom of all these issues. But none of them is central to the actor's task.

If that is truly the case, then what is?

The answer concerns action. You must always be focused on questions about the action of the script. And that means plot—that's right, the insulting, obvious part of discussing literature. The part we take for granted—at least when it's done effectively. And we're used to doing so because the literature and film that's considered worthy of study *does* render the story effectively. Keep in mind that every shot, every angle, every edit in a successful film is a choice thought through and executed to make the overall story clear and compelling. This is not easy to do. It only seems so when done well. And that same task—to make the story clear and compelling—is your primary task as an actor.

In the well-told story, everything that's said is there for a reason, and everything that's in the story is placed just where it needs to be. And that is exactly how you must approach your task as an actor. The questions you must first and primarily focus on are questions that relate to what is happening in the story. The questions you want to be asking are not philosophical; they are practical. You'll want to be asking questions like these:

- What are the events of the story?
- How does one event lead to the next event?
- What are the triggers that lead from one event to another?
- What is my character's responsibility in creating and moving through those events?
- What must my character be doing to make those events clear and compelling?
- What things must my character do to make the story clear?
- What things must my character do to make the character clear and compelling?

27

- How should my character do these things physically and through the dialogue to make the character and story he or she is charged with telling clear and compelling?

Is this the way you are currently thinking about your work as an actor? I bet it's not.

In Chapter One, we reviewed many of the basic elements and concepts that make up an actor's tool kit. We talked conflict, objectives, tactics, given circumstances, etc. If you take a moment now and think about the long list of items in that tool kit, you will probably find that most of them relate directly or indirectly to the action of the story. The word drama itself, by the way, comes from the Greek word that means *action*. None of this is accidental. The playwright is a storyteller; the actor is, too. And all storytelling is about the action of the story. Yes, we need characters to do the action, and dialogue helps make that action clear, but the bottom line is that even character-centered stories are driven by action. This means that your primary responsibility must be to know what that action is and to carry it out effectively.

In several books and articles I have written over the years—some of which your teachers may have forced upon you—I have defined good acting in the following way:

Good acting is acting that is believable and tells the best possible story while serving the script.

It is my belief that if you get in the habit of considering all of the elements in this three-pronged definition before you start rehearsing, your work as an actor is far more likely to be successful.

Here's what I mean.

The first element in the definition is the part that most actors put all their effort into: the task of being believable. This is not the same as what we call realism (a style of writing or acting in which the characters look and sound like actual people from the world where we live). What is believable in a contemporary realistic work may not be believable when doing Shakespeare or Molière. Their plays are language-centered, and telling their stories believably means paying extra attention to the language and learning to use it effectively. You've probably seen some American actors in Shakespeare films (with otherwise British casts) who don't seem to cut it. Even though they're good actors, they just don't seem believable in this context, usually because their realistic style doesn't fit into the world of the play. If you're not quite sure what I'm talking about here, check out Al Pacino's documentary film *Looking for Richard*, or watch Kevin Costner in his version of *Robin Hood*, where he plays opposite Alan Rickman (of *Harry Potter* Snape fame). You'll soon know exactly what I'm talking about.

Most of the acting that you are called upon to do, however, will be in the style of realism. Most contemporary plays are written with dialogue that is meant to sound just as people in real life today actually sound. I like to tell my own students that they will know when their work is believable when a stranger walks into the studio while they're working, and the intruders can't tell whether the actors are acting or being themselves. Many fine film and television actors rely on doing just that. They know how to look and sound just like contemporary human beings. As you've probably discovered, that in itself is no easy task. But it is not always enough, especially when you're working on the stage.

That brings us to the next prong in the definition: to tell the best possible story. As an actor, you have the obligation to tell the story of the play and your character clearly and effectively. While you are maintaining your believability, you must also make choices that tell the audience what they need to know in terms of the story and your character. You have only the lines and what you do physically to make that happen. How you say your lines and what you choose to do tell the audience what you're thinking and feeling from moment to moment. That means your actions should never be random. They should result from choices you make. An audience doesn't know what you are thinking and feeling. They cannot get into your mind and heart. What they know about you comes from what you tell them—through your physical choices and through what you do with the dialogue. It is up to you to make the story clear.

But believability and clarity are still not enough. You must also make the story as exciting as possible. If you and that other actor called back for a final audition are equally believable, who will get the job? In all probability, all other things being equal, it will be the actor who is more interesting. Making your character and the story you are telling as compelling as possible is also part of your job. This is as much about choices as it is about personal charisma or energy. You must understand your storytelling obligations if you are going to make choices that tell the overall story in an exciting way.

And that's the trick that leads to the third prong of the definition of good acting. Exciting, compelling choices are wonderful. But those choices must be in the service of the script. Have you ever gone to see a production of a famous play where all the actors seem believable and exciting, and all their choices seem absolutely clear—and yet the play doesn't seem to work, or even make sense? And you're left with the thought, "Why is this play so famous? It doesn't even work!"

If you have had such an experience, chances are some of the actors in that production had not made choices that serve the script. In other words, what they chose to do was at the expense of how the script was actually intended to function. Maybe the evil villain didn't scare you because he was downright likable. Or the male lead came off as mean to his romantic counterpart, so we didn't root for the couple to get together. Or all the characters were jealous of the pretty new girl in town, but we in the audience never fell under her spell. On the assumption that each of these productions was properly cast, in all likelihood, the failure of the finished product was a result of poor choices on the actors' parts. Choices were made that failed to serve the script.

Of course, you may be thinking that all this is the director's fault, because he or she is charged with putting all the pieces of the production together effectively. And that is true, up to a point. But most actors with a lot of professional experience will tell you that there aren't that many actors' directors out there, and much of the time professional actors are left largely to their own devices. In the end, it is you that the audience sees—whether the choices you play are your own or the director's. You must, during your actor training, learn to be director proof. You must learn to do the analysis and make your choices independently.

Recently, I taught a graduate course to theatre civilians called From Page to Stage, about choice-making in the theatre. We read famous plays and discussed how theatre practitioners analyze scripts for production—why they make the choices they make. During a unit on *Fences*, the iconic play by August Wilson, I showed excerpts from various performances I had found on YouTube. I was able to find several clips from the original Broadway production, for which James Earl Jones won a Tony Award for his performance as Troy Maxson. I was also able to find clips from the recent Broadway revival that starred Denzel Washington and Viola Davis. There were literally scores of other clips from a host of productions that ranged from professional to amateur. Watching many different realizations of just one scene, the students quickly grasped how the three-pronged definition of good acting intersects with the making of a successful work on stage. I strongly suggest you do this kind of exploration yourself. It will quickly bring home the major points of this chapter thus far. Some of our observations from the class will give you an idea of what I mean.

No one would deny that James Earl Jones and Denzel Washington are both superb actors. Their work on stage and screen is consistently of the highest caliber. Their believability, the first prong in the definition of good acting, never comes into question. But these actors are also very different. James Earl Jones, with his size and booming voice, has had more success on stage than in the movies, his voice role as Darth Vader not withstanding. He has a larger-than-life charisma that on the stage becomes mesmerizing in the right roles. His legendary performances in *The Great White Hope*, *Othello*, and *Fences* support this point.

In *Fences*, Jones parlayed his physical and vocal stature into making the character of Troy an almost godlike presence. He accomplished this despite the fact that August Wilson's script portrays Troy mostly as a failure—as a husband, as a father, as a brother, and as a friend. Troy struggles with his failings, and he struggles as a black man in a northern industrial city of the 1950s. But the combination of Jones's personality and his skillful choices made the character an almost tragic hero that perfectly supported the themes invoked by the playwright. The story of Troy and his family worked beautifully. Though set in Pittsburgh, the play seemed almost classical and epic. Jones's choices told the best possible story and served the script brilliantly.

Jones's performance is a tough act to follow, especially considering that many of the people who saw the original production of *Fences* are still around to remember it. Though Denzel Washington is a powerful stage presence in his own right, he doesn't create the kind of Olympian effect on stage that Jones did as Troy. Besides, he obviously did not want to be accused of doing an imitation of what Jones had brought to the role. And so, as a fine actor, he decided to go in a completely different direction.

Washington's choices produced a Troy who was far more down-to-earth and far less imposing. He was warmer and funnier and more playful. He was more likable and less dangerous. The play's themes and story were still clear and compelling, but the production was far less memorable, and "epic" would not have been a word that came to mind. For my money, Washington's performance was excellent—he was believable and served the script. But for me, that "to tell the best possible story" prong of the definition of good acting was not quite achieved. The urgency and stakes that James Earl Jones brought to the role have probably not been matched to this day. I am not in any way faulting Mr. Washington. He remains one of my favorite actors. I am simply trying to make the point that each of those prongs in the definition of good acting is essential. And that learning to analyze and synthesize choices is every bit as important to the acting process as believability.

I mentioned that there were many other clips from productions of *Fences* readily available. If for one moment you feel tempted to take for granted the excellent work of Mr. Jones and Mr. Washington, I strongly suggest that you watch some excerpts from other productions in addition to the ones you find with these great actors. You will quickly come to appreciate the artistry that this duo brings to the role. And you will quickly realize that the three-pronged definition of good acting will serve you well as both mantra and compass in your quest to build your own good acting.

Here is another example that you can easily check out online. Look for scenes from productions of the classic Arthur Miller play *Death of Salesman*, particularly the clips with Lee J. Cobb, the original Willy Loman, and with his most famous Loman rival, Dustin Hoffman. The latter played the role on Broadway in the 1980s. The late Phillip Seymour Hoffman also took on the role more recently in a lauded production directed by Mike Nichols, but clips from that production are as of this writing still hard to find.

What you will see from Lee J. Cobb are the kind of choices that James Earl Jones brought to *Fences*. Cobb's performance also turns the title character into an almost tragic hero who, though a failure in terms of the classic definition of American success, continues to rage against the forces that have kept him down. Like a Greek hero of old, his Willy refuses to accept his fate. Interestingly, there are several accounts of this seminal production directed by Elia Kazan that report that Arthur Miller himself saw Willy Loman as a small and defeated character. But as Cobb's interpretation developed and Kazan's direction supported that approach, Miller apparently rewrote some dialogue to accommodate this interpretation. When Dustin Hoffman took on the role, he decided, no doubt because of his own physical stature, to return the vision of Willy to Miller's original concept of the character. With Miller's support and approval, Dustin Hoffman's performance, though somewhat controversial, received high praise and created tremendous interest in the production. It also generated a new wave of admiration for Arthur Miller and his body of work.

If you watch both productions in their entirety back to back (and they are readily available), you will see two very different plays. The choices that the actors playing Willy must make affect all the choices of the other characters as well. A strong Willy creates a need for a different kind of strength from his son Biff and his wife, Linda. A weak Willy Loman creates an entirely different set of possibilities, as a young John Malkovich in the Dustin Hoffman version will quickly demonstrate. But the play that Miller wrote is so powerful and so universal that it can accommodate a huge range of choices that will still allow the work to maintain its brilliance and universality. Unfortunately, as you scan your YouTube offerings, you will also discover an almost infinite number of choices that simply don't work. As you watch, keep in mind that definition of good acting. You'll be able to see that three-pronged definition play out again and again for better or for worse.

So, the answer to how you make choices that are believable, tell the best possible story, and serve the script goes back to analysis. You simply have to learn to read a play for how it works before you can make the choices as an actor that will ensure that it does. You will have to learn to recognize how your part in the script contributes to the machinery the good playwright has given you. This is a skill that must be practiced repeatedly if you are going to master it. It is a skill that must be developed through your willingness to learn to ask the right questions, and to take the time to figure out the best answers. All this takes discipline and commitment. The good news here is that if you master the ability to analyze and make good choices, the likelihood of your producing consistently believable and exciting work increases exponentially.

In Chapter Three, we'll take a more in-depth look at some of the questions you must ask yourself if you're going to analyze a play successfully. Asking these questions will help you begin the journey toward effective storytelling choices, both for the action of the play and for your character. We will also begin to develop this process by looking at a few familiar stories in the analytical way that you as an actor must.

CHAPTER THREE

Making Good Choices

In the first two chapters of this book, we examined the actor's tool kit and the definition of good acting. You learned that both the tools found in that tool kit and the three-pronged definition of what an actor must do are, at their core, concerned with helping the actor communicate the playwright's story. Each will help you as an actor find and make choices that will make you believable and compelling. But, as you have also learned, more than anything else your job as an actor centers on being a good storyteller. You must understand how the story works, and how to make choices for your character that contribute to your overall storytelling responsibilities. You have learned that good analysis leads to good choices and good choices lead to clear, compelling stories. You have also learned that playing a character must never come at the expense of your overall storytelling obligations, and that your primary function is to effectively carry out your part in telling that overall story.

Unfortunately, the untrained or improperly trained actor tends to think of herself as the center of focus and not as a piece of the puzzle that must fit perfectly into the composition of the entire picture. It is important to keep in mind that before any specific choices about character can be made, you must be able to visualize the story contained in the play from the point of view of the audience, and remember the structure of the play you are serving. You must first look at the play from some distance so that you can take in the whole story, event by event, and not just from the point of view of your character.

Focusing on what the audience needs to see will help you begin thinking about your character in terms of chosen actions rather than creating persona. It is essential to keep in mind that your character does not exist outside of the script. Your character exists because the playwright needed that character to be there—to serve his purposes, not yours.

Once you understand how the play works dramatically as a whole, you can begin to focus on the development of your individual character—in service of the script. Developing a character to play on the stage, or on the screen for that matter, will involve working with the following ingredients:

- The playwright's vision, suggested mostly through words
- The physical, intellectual, and emotional presence of the actor cast in the role
- The choices that actor makes for that role—physically, psychologically, and emotionally
- The physical manner in which the actor carries out those choices

When you think about it, it is no wonder that no two Troy Maxsons or Willy Lomans are ever exactly alike. To some extent, an actor plays herself in every role she takes on, since it is only through your own intellectual, emotional, physical, and experiential makeup that you can understand and communicate the character you portray. But you must never forget that your first step in the process of finding and developing a character is to understand your obligations to the story set down in the script. By doing so, you ensure that your choices will lead you in the right direction.

In Chapters One and Two, you also learned that actions, which include all the things a character says and does physically, are the tangible aspects of any performance. Only through what is tangible will an audience ultimately come to know who a character is. An audience cannot read a character's mind or look into a character's heart. An audience can only make assumptions and draw conclusions from what it sees and hears. Obviously, then, the actions you choose to present to an audience are extremely important. As noted in Chapter Two, the actions you select and perform are mostly generated as a result of:

- Understanding the story you are telling
- Understanding the mechanics of that story
- Making choices based on that understanding that will clarify the action of the overall story and of your character
- Understanding how the character you are playing fits into that overall story
- Making choices for your character that further that overall story as well as that of your character
- Making choices that clarify the story of your character in terms of who you are and why you do the things you do
- Making choices at every moment that reveal what you are thinking and feeling as a character to the degree that the script demands

By finding and playing actions that come out of your analysis, you will create an arc or throughline of action for your character. This arc will not only define your character moment by moment and scene by scene; it will also suggest the changes that your character undergoes in the time that elapses between each scene. This process of creating complexity through simplicity may seem like cheating, but working in this manner is far more reliable than trying to magically "become the character."

Now that you are armed with your definition of good acting and a set of bullet points that will help keep you on track, let's take a look at some stories that you are probably familiar with, just to get a feel for the mind-set an actor needs when approaching a script. By the time we have finished our examination, you will probably have very different perceptions of these works, despite the fact that they have been part of your universe since words started having meaning to you.

Let's start with "Goldilocks and the Three Bears," a story you've probably heard too many times to count. The first question you may want to ask yourself as an actor in overview terms is, "What is the actual story here?" For our purposes, let's define *story* as a recounting of the sequence of events that involves a particular group of characters. So, if we break the question down further, we are asking, "What are the chronological events of this story?" You may want to take a moment now to actually recount the chronological events to yourself. You may even want to jot those events down. Then continue reading.

This little exercise likely proved to be more challenging than you first thought it would be. Perhaps as you were writing your sequence of events you found yourself going back to add information or actions that were crucial to the story but had been left out of the chronology. You may have had to rearrange some events as well in order for the story to make sense—in order for the cause-and-effect logic to work.

As a result of undertaking this task, you probably found yourself thinking about the action of the story more deeply and specifically than you usually do. Having heard the tale probably countless times in childhood, you may not have considered until now that it is a pretty strange story, and in some ways not a very interesting one. While it can certainly give rise to many questions, they aren't profound philosophical questions about the meaning of the story or the motivations of the characters or what it all says about the human condition. I mean basic questions about what the story is and how the story works.

This exercise, by the way, is an analogy for the kind of analysis you really need to be doing as an actor with a real script. Very often our literature classes train us to look deeply for the meaning of the story or what the characters tell us about who we are as human beings. And yes, ultimately it is good for us as actors to have that kind of awareness. But our primary job is to find specific actions to play that get the story across to the audience. Our job is to break the story down to its simplest and most necessary actions so that we can figure out what exactly and precisely we need to do when we're on stage to get the story across. It is the playwright's job to go deep and make universal statements, and the good playwright has probably done so. But when we select the right simple actions to play, the story and its meaning will come across to an audience. Our job is to maximize the story the playwright has given us. That means making it believable, clear, and as exciting as possible.

In the first chapter, we talked a lot about conflict, the engine of drama. All good stories start with conflict. Plots are built on it. Objectives that you must play as an actor are determined by that conflict. And person-versus-person conflict is the most useful kind of conflict to an actor, because you are always looking for the conflict between you and the actors you share the stage with. Playwrights write with that principle in mind.

So, as you look over your sequence of events in the story of the three bears, think about conflict. Think about the person-versus-person conflict or conflicts found in the tale of those three furry creatures and the blonde kid. Take a moment now and do so.

What you probably discovered is that "Goldilocks and the Three Bears" is not exactly filled with the "c" word. There is not much conflict—not between the characters, at least. In some versions of the story Goldilocks barely has any contact with the bears. The bears discover her, and she's quickly out of bed and out the window. Not much person-versus-person conflict in that. The bears don't really have any genuine conflicts with each other, either. They don't argue about the comfort of the various chairs, the relative warmth of their individual bowls of porridge, or which bed is the best for sleeping. They simply report to each other on the qualities they discover regarding each of the items. Maybe this is why most people I polled did not choose this story as a favorite. The story is simply weak on conflict.

But that is not the end of the story, so to speak. There are still elements in the tale that actors can use to maximize its limited story-telling potential. It becomes your job to recognize those elements, so that your eventual choices will make maximum use of what's there—or, rather, what you discover is there. That again is why you must learn to analyze effectively. Remember, particularly in the beginning of your acting career if you choose to pursue one, you'll be mostly cast in untested new works. Some of them will be good; many of them will not. If you need the work, you'll take the job anyway. You should take the job. Working is better than not working. But it will be on you to find your way through the bad material and make a good showing. Learning how to maximize what the script offers will be essential.

So if there isn't much person-versus-person conflict, what is there to work with? Let's start with the bears. Now, if I were writing a new version of the story, I would find a way to use the bowls of porridge, the chairs, and the beds to create some kind of conflict within the bear family. But as actors we can't do this. We can't change the script. We must work with what we have. In most versions of the story, the bears don't deal with the beds and chairs until after Goldilocks has disturbed them. The bears establish who they are at the kitchen table with their porridge only. Each of the bears gets a moment with his or her bowl to determine whether the porridge is ready to be devoured. Aside from its temperature, we know nothing about the porridge. Is it delicious, bland, or awful? Making some choices will give us some storytelling options. Does the porridge need sugar, or salt, or maybe some honey? If it does, is the salt, honey, or sugar readily available and easy to apply? The answer should be no. You can always flavor the story with obstacles to make the situation more interesting. You should always be asking yourself where you can find some conflict and some obstacles to enhance the story.

What if Baby Bear wants honey for the porridge, but it's kept in a large jar that he can barely reach? What if Mama Bear has to get the sugar and she can't get the new bag open? What if Papa knocks the saltshaker and it spills all over the table? Would it provide more conflict if the porridge is delicious, or if it's awful? You've got to think through the possibilities. Suppose it's delicious, but too hot to eat? Papa could be conflicted between his bearlike appetite and burning himself. Baby Bear might not be able to control himself at all and could end up burning his tongue. Or perhaps the bears hate the taste of the porridge, which would play very differently. Without adding dialogue, the actors playing these roles could physically act out these possibilities to show character and make the story more interesting.

When Goldilocks checks out the porridge, chairs, and beds, she too has an opportunity to show who she is by how she reacts to everything. If the actor playing Goldilocks thinks in terms of obstacles and internal conflicts, there is a whole clan of unbearably interesting things she could do to enhance the bare bones of the story provided. By way of example, she could rock 'til she drops. As her rocking in Baby's chair gets wilder, the audience will start to worry that Goldi might hurt herself or, worse, break the chair. She might bounce on the bed and build that action from calm to frenzied on each of the three beds. This would create a series of story arcs that would be fun and create tension. More importantly, if the actor playing Goldilocks established that she was aware that the owners might return at any time and checked for them periodically, she would create a good deal of suspense while on her path of destruction.

And, speaking of suspense, the manner in which the bears discover Goldilocks could become a tension-filled story arc as well. Consider: as the bears move from room to room discovering and formulating evidence, they slowly reach the conclusion that an intruder may still be present. How could you show this without adding dialogue? Classic Hitchcock, right? Would you consider these possibilities on your own? Good actors do. Here's another angle: what is Goldi doing while the bears are downstairs? Is she sleeping soundly the entire time? What is the best moment for her to wake up? Does she wake up slowly, so that the bears burst in before she's ready to size up the situation? Or is it a better storytelling choice for her to simply sit up startled, then jump out of bed and fly out the window? Is it easy to get out the window? Often it is portrayed that way. Is that the best storytelling choice? Or would there be a good conflict/obstacle available to use if the window did not cooperate? These are all questions that you might consider as your analysis leads you to your storytelling possibilities.

Obviously, there are countless other possibilities to be discovered and considered. For the moment, we are looking at the script at a distance—from the perspective of the audience, trying to see the best possibilities for unfolding the story effectively. The close work comes later. The important point here is whether you think this way when you are examining a script. If you don't, I hope I've made the case that it is something that you should learn to do.

Now let's look at another story, by way of contrast—"The Three Little Pigs." In this story there is a big and obvious person-versus-person conflict to work with. The conflict begins to develop almost immediately, at least as it is portrayed in some versions—when the mama pig warns her children that the houses they build must be strong if they are to survive the attacks of a hungry and determined wolf. Each of the pigs is given an opportunity in the story to go through some internal conflict when deciding what kind of house to build. If the version you know centers on the conflict between laziness and doing things right, then each of the pigs has an even more specific internal conflict to work with in the process of selecting building materials. If the script allows, each pig will have an opportunity to show who he is by his selection of materials and by the manner in which he constructs his house. Is he meticulous or careless? Are his rhythms and tempos fast or slow? Is he more concerned about building fast or well? Remember, character is demonstrated through action. What you do and how you do it will help tell both the story of the play and the story of your character. Further, the choices you make should serve the overall story, not simply define your character as you'd like to play him.

When the wolf comes to the door, there is dramatic, life-and-death conflict. What choices could you make as an actor playing each of the pigs to show who you are and to maximize the story potential? Keep in mind that there is a sequence of repetition here as well. The wolf visits each house—and the story must continue to build through each step in the sequence to reach a satisfying storytelling climax and conclusion. In other words, the wolf blowing down the first two houses should be as suspenseful as possible, but the second should create more tension than the first. And the visit to the third house, that one of brick, must be the most gripping of all if the plot line is going to be maximized. What choices should you make if your character is going to be clear and compelling? How do these choices support and magnify the overall story being told? They must do both.

And finally, what about the wolf? Who is he? Is he a moustache-twirling villain, or does he have levels? In part, this will be determined by the script. But if the script allows the wolf to be more than a one-dimensional salivating monster, what conflicts and obstacles might you be able to invent for him without diminishing the potential for terror? It is your job to maximize that conflict, to invent moment-to-moment tension in your scenes with each of those pigs—and of course to be as scary as possible.

Now let's take a moment with Red Riding Hood and the gang. This story deals with subtler themes and actions than the previous two, so the way it is written and the way it is played will powerfully shape the audience's understanding of the tale. Is this story meant to be funny? Is it meant to be scary? Both? How do you as the actor serve the script? Here are just a few other things to think about. What exactly is Red's objective in this story, and when, where, and how do her objectives change? Why does that happen? How does it happen? Is Red an intelligent, determined girl with a streak of rebel in her? Or is she a sweet, attractive but not-too-bright waif, ripe for picking? Or is she something in between? What does the script you are using suggest? Which makes for the best story? What choices best justify the action and its progression in the particular version you are acting in?

And here are a few questions about the wolf. Is he pure menace? Or is he a charmer who can turn vicious? Why and how does he manage to get Red to talk to him in the woods? What objectives and tactics will be needed? Does he use pressure and fear? Or is he a charming, attractive, feral creature? What does the script tell you? What characteristics do you possess as an actor that will make it all work? What exactly do you want from Red, anyway? If she's just a meal for you, why don't you make a lunch of her here in the woods? Why the race to Grandmother's house, and all the nonsense that follows?

Of course, when we first read this tale or, more likely, had it read to us, none of these kinds of questions even occurred to us. We were lost in the story and let it carry us along, shortcomings and unanswered questions notwithstanding. The vague theatre of our minds accepted the story as presented. But once we are charged with telling that story, we are required to make choices as actors playing those characters—choices that justify what those characters do and forward the story believably and compellingly. And how does the woodsman fit into the whole deal, anyway?

There are many simple tales that you could examine in the manner we have just undertaken. You may want to try a couple on your own. We have certainly left a number of loose ends with "Little Red Riding Hood." Each new tale you take on will provide you with a new set of problems to address and solve. Remember, repetition is one of the keys to developing your analysis skills. I certainly hope that at this point you buy into its usefulness to you as an actor.

Asking the right questions and coming up with the right answers can only help you in your quest to be as good as you can be. In time you will discover how difficult it is to be believable when you are making choices or playing actions that do not serve the script. It is always part of your job to understand the story being told so that you can clearly tell and, hopefully, enhance the story the playwright has given you. Remember, the compelling story that you tell through your chosen actions must never come at the expense of the story the playwright has provided.

Believe me, I realize that some of the answers to some of the questions raised in this chapter might be answered as a result of table discussion with a director, or discovered during the rehearsal process. But the realities of American theater (and film, for that matter) are such that rehearsal times are short and directors expect that you will come to the first rehearsal—and all rehearsals thereafter—prepared and armed with choices and ideas that will enhance your own work and help the overall production. Analysis and good choices are part of your job, whether they have been a part of your training as an actor or not. My suggestion is to start practicing these skills immediately. They will provide you with an unshakable brick house to live in throughout your career.

CHAPTER FOUR

◇◇

Starting Your
Detective Work

So far we have discussed the tools of craft and how to apply them in general terms to the story being told. We have discussed the definition of good acting and how it relates to that story. We have explored the concept of character through action, and we have learned that the actions we choose to play, both in terms of acting objective and physicality, must come from our analysis of the story we are serving. But we have done all this by referencing the story in a general sense only.

Now it's time for us to take the next step: the exploration of an actual script, where the words the playwright has painstakingly put to paper must be analyzed and synthesized. Are you ready now to begin the specific detective work that is required of you as an actor? If so, you will have to sift through the dialogue and implied action the playwright has set down and find the clues to clear and compelling acting choices—choices that serve the playwright's vision and your storytelling obligations.

Before we begin our exploration, let's consider a few basic concepts that will be essential to your ability to analyze and synthesize effectively:

- The story is what holds a play together.
- The story consists of its characters, its action, its dialogue, and the manner in which that story is told.
- The manner in which it is told includes the story's tone and narrative viewpoint.
- No individual ingredient can ever be more important than its combination of parts. No audience would come to see a play just to watch an individual character, any more than they might eat a cake for the eggs that are in it.
- An audience wants to see characters in the context of a play's action. And few characters and fewer performances are so compelling, so absorbing, or so amusing that an audience will commit to watching them for two hours unless they are also engaged by the question of what is going to happen next.

Playwrights want their work to be successful. They know story is essential. Therefore, if you read a play and can't find the story to hang your choices on, there is either a problem with the play or a problem with your reading of it. If the play you're working on is an established one, then you know where the problem lies. But even when the play is a poor one, or its storyline is weak, it is still your job to make the most out of what you are given to work with. And, because rehearsal periods are usually too short for extended exploration, you will be expected to show up to work with the goods in hand. You will need to know how to prepare on your own.

In this chapter, we will practice asking the necessary questions of the script and of the playwright who wrote that script. If you begin with the premise that everything the playwright has written into her script is there for a reason, you will have the motivation to take everything you see on the printed page as a clue to doing your job as an actor effectively.

Some of the elements you will have to think about, certainly at the beginning stages of your analysis, include the following:

- **given circumstances**—the who, what, when, and where of the play. The more specifically you define them, the more specific your choices will become. Choices that are specific are more likely to be clear and compelling. Generalized choices will not be.
- **story**—the narrative produced when character, plot, and dialogue are combined, producing a particular effect, feeling, idea, or all three.
- **arc or throughline**—the map of the journey a character makes through a story. It can be literal or figurative in that it marks the changes a character undergoes during the course of the action and provides moments that are dramatic and revealing.
- **conflict**—the engine of drama, created when the opposing forces that make a story interesting square off.
- **objective**—what the character needs and pursues at all times, resulting from the conflict the playwright creates.
- **moments**—specific islands of import in the story's progression or arc; places in the script where moments can be made, revealed, and/or portrayed dramatically. Victories, defeats, and discoveries are often made there.
- **physical actions**—the things the actor chooses to do physically to make thought and feelings clear.

We'll take a look at all these items more closely a bit later, but for now let's just work on an overview.

Below you will find an excerpt from the one-act play *Ten-Dollar Drinks*, by Joe Pintauro. The play consists of a conversation between two women over drinks in a famous and very expensive restaurant. At the time the play was written, a "ten-dollar drink" was a pricey one indeed. Needless to say, before you can make any decisions about the characters and action, it will be necessary to read and understand the entire play and how the pieces work together; but for the purposes of this exercise, let's assume that what appears below is the entire work. Without any further information from me, then, read the excerpt below and see what you can learn about the given circumstances (the who, what, when, and where of the script) in spite of not having the whole play to work with. Just use what you find below and see what you can come up with. As you read, you should underline, highlight, or jot down phrases that give you clues.

Once you have accumulated your list, go back over it and think about the significance of each clue you chose to list. We'll compare notes after you have completed your investigation. Read the excerpt as many times as you want or need to. Remember, multiple, careful readings are essential to an actor trying to accumulate necessary information. Consider yourself a detective on the case.

<><><><><><><><><><><><><><><><><><><><><><><><><><><><><><><><><>

TEN-DOLLAR DRINKS

Characters:
STAR—thirty or over
BETE—thirty or over

Star is extremely well dressed, Bete, less so.

Setting:
A drinks table at the Russian Tea Room.

STAR   I mean *everyone* was there. Everyone.

BETE   The only stars I give a damn about are the ones on my kid's report card.

STAR   How is he...uh...

BETE   You forgot his name.

STAR   Jesse.

BETE   You forgot before you remembered. Just the way you saw me that night at Allison's, and lousy actress that you are you screwed up pretending not to see me.

STAR   I saw you at Allison's.

BETE   You are the worst.

STAR   I was surrounded by twenty sycophantic moving mouths.

BETE   Congratulations! Congratulations! But meantime we waited on your leash for you to say hi...

STAR   I had another party to go to.

BETE   We figured as much, my dear, but we refused to suffer the ignominy of you leaving first and waving us a pathetic *"Dear, what can I do?"*

STAR   Talk about your son. That calms you.

BETE   He got into Trinity.

STAR   I presume that's good news.

BETE   In my world it is.

STAR   Well, that's nice.

BETE   Till my money runs out. And don't you interpret that as I got you here to ask for a handout.

STAR   Thanks. Here's to Jesse.

BETE   That I'll drink to.

STAR   Why'd you pick a place where the drinks are ten bucks?

BETE   Me, invite a star to a no-class joint?

STAR   I'll pick up the check if you let me.

BETE   You bet your sweet ass I'll let you.

STAR   What about all that voice-over work?

BETE   New producer, new voice. Yesterday I got a call for a denture spot.

STAR   You didn't.

BETE   Old people are getting younger every day, honey.

STAR   In L.A. they said you're up for that Pinter thing.

BETE   Yeah.

STAR   Tired?

BETE   Just pissed. At my husband for being a drunk, my parents for dying, the dying was bad enough but leaving me shit…,

STAR   Uh….What the hell time is it?

BETE   Now tell me you've got to go.

STAR   No, go on…your husband?

BETE   I went and fell in love with an actor who hates himself, what else is new, except this one's a drunk so I go ahead and have his kid.

STAR   You're talkin' about your son now.

BETE   A terrific kid, knock wood.

STAR   Does he see his dad?

BETE   From a cab a couple weeks ago we saw him in rotted jogging shoes with glassy eyes, walking his dog.

STAR   I thought he got himself a soap.

BETE   He's on the "World" thing or "The Bold and the Broken."

STAR   Then he should help with Jesse.

BETE   He sends some money. (STAR *stares as if to ask,* "*Then why kvetch?*")

STAR I hate to say this, but I got a damn P.R. meeting.
So... what is it? I showed up. So?

BETE Okay. I'm not jealous of you.

STAR That's it?

BETE Before we drift apart, as we obviously will, and
you decide you don't know me at all anymore, I want it
in the record that I'll never envy you no matter what
you accumulate, acquire...

STAR You've got too much on the ball to envy anybody.

BETE True.

STAR Too bad the rest of the world hasn't acknowledged
this.

BETE That's okay... (*The insult catches up to her.*) Let's
keep it between you and me, shall we? (*Now letting it
show.*) I'm not ashamed to look you in the eye and
show you the hurt I feel.

STAR Hurt for yourself or me?

BETE Hurt that you walk around this town like you
never knew a lot of your old friends.

STAR Oh, Jesus.

BETE Oh, Jesus, huh?

STAR I win that cursed thing and suddenly I need four
telephones and still I have to hire someone around the
apartment to screen my callers. I hear from high-school
friends, relatives I never met. I'm a freak. I'm worn out...

BETE We acted in the same company for ten years. We
ate more dinners, spent more rotten hours together. I
paid for more coffees. We slept together more nights...

STAR You're not going around claiming that.

BETE You dog. I meant I had to put you to sleep, you
drunk, on my couch a half dozen times. I'm not

55

claiming to be your sister or some high-school jerk. You always were using everyone, everything. And it worked. What are you complaining about? So here's to your fucking obese ego, your obscene Oscar and your fame. (STAR *pushes her drink away.*)

STAR You know what fame is? Multiply all the people you don't wanna know by two hundred million. That's fame. Fame...is the drink that comes to your table from that dark corner of the restaurant and it could be from either a deranged stalker or your future lover. Either way if you don't drink the shit they'll hate you till they die. There is nothing spiritual about fame. Fame is prostitution without body contact. I know only one person who believed she was a true goddess. She refused to go to the bathroom because it would destroy her status and she wound up exploding in a Los Angeles emergency room. That's fame, honey.

BETE Well, it didn't look that way at the Academy Awards.

STAR (*With fear of the jealousy and the punishment.*) Did you watch?

BETE You looked great. You said exactly the right thing. I was proud.

STAR But did you watch?

BETE Well, of course I watched.

◇◇

If you didn't compile your own list, examine the one below and see if you can determine why I included the items I did. If you have compiled a list, compare yours to the one that follows and see if you can figure out why there are differences. There are no rights or wrongs here, only pieces of information that will help us understand the characters and the story and, later, to make choices—choices that will help tell the story effectively.

What do the items on the lists tell us about Star and Bete? About their relationship? About their history together? About their lives currently? About their feelings toward each other? About their values? What do they tell us about the current situation? What changes occur during the conversation that affect the answers to these questions? Are the characters different at the end of the excerpt than they are at the beginning? Or have your perceptions of them changed? Examine these changes and try to determine what they tell us about the story, about the characters. What is the tone of the piece? Is it funny? Dramatic? A combination? And so on.

Here are my clues:

> STAR—thirty or over
> BETE—thirty or over
> Star is extremely well dressed, Bete, less so.
> A drinks table at the Russian Tea Room.
> STAR I mean *everyone* was there. Everyone.
> BETE The only stars I give a damn about are the ones on my kid's report card.
> STAR Talk about your son. That calms you.
> BETE Till my money runs out. And don't you interpret that as I got you here to ask for a handout.
> STAR Why'd you pick a place where the drinks are ten bucks?
> STAR I'll pick up the check if you let me.
> BETE You bet your sweet ass I'll let you.
> BETE Yesterday I got a call for a denture spot.

BETE Just pissed. At my husband for being a drunk, my parents for dying, the dying was bad enough but leaving me shit...

BETE I went and fell in love with an actor who hates himself, what else is new, except this one's a drunk so I go ahead and have his kid.

BETE From a cab a couple weeks ago we saw him in rotted jogging shoes with glassy eyes, walking his dog.

BETE He's on the "World" thing or "The Bold and the Broken."

BETE Okay. I'm not jealous of you.

BETE Before we drift apart, as we obviously will, and you decide you don't know me at all anymore, I want it in the record that I'll never envy you no matter what you accumulate, acquire...

STAR You've got too much on the ball to envy anybody.

BETE Hurt that you walk around this town like you never knew a lot of your old friends.

STAR I win that cursed thing and suddenly I need four telephones and still I have to hire someone around the apartment to screen my callers. I hear from high-school friends, relatives I never met. I'm a freak. I'm worn out...

BETE We acted in the same company for ten years. We ate more dinners, spent more rotten hours together. I paid for more coffees. We slept together more nights...

BETE You dog. I meant I had to put you to sleep, you drunk, on my couch a half dozen times. I'm not claiming to be your sister or some high-school jerk. You always were using everyone, everything. And it worked. What are you complaining about? So here's to your

fucking obese ego, your obscene Oscar and your fame.
(STAR *pushes her drink away.*)

STAR   You know what fame is? Multiply all the people
you don't wanna know by two hundred million. That's
fame. Fame...is the drink that comes to your table
from that dark corner of the restaurant and it could be
from either a deranged stalker or your future lover.
Either way if you don't drink the shit they'll hate you
till they die. There is nothing spiritual about fame.
Fame is prostitution without body contact. I know only
one person who believed she was a true goddess. She
refused to go to the bathroom because it would destroy
her status and she wound up exploding in a Los Angeles
emergency room. That's fame, honey.

BETE   Well, it didn't look that way at the Academy
Awards.

STAR   (*With fear of the jealousy and the punishment.*) Did
you watch?

BETE   You looked great. You said exactly the right thing.
I was proud.

Notice that my clues came both from the dialogue and from the stage
directions. It is fair and wise to use everything available for your analysis. My list could have been far longer. In fact, I might have included
everything in the script. The fact is, everything in a good script is
there for a reason. Further, as I noted earlier, actions implied or explicit in a script can be every bit as useful for analysis as dialogue. We
can sometimes learn about a play's story and its characters through
what the author tells us directly through commentary and stage direction. More often, however, we learn through what the characters
say, through what they do, and through what other characters say

about them. The two longer speeches by Star and Bete near the end of the cutting are particularly telling. How many clues to characters and situation can you find in these two speeches alone? Several paragraphs could probably be composed using only these speeches. It might be a worthwhile exercise to note from my list above or from your own which clues are based on what the characters actually say, which ones are based on what they do, and which ones are based on what the other characters says about them. You will notice that each category yields equally important clues, and literally all things said and done should be examined actively.

All right, now that you've collected your information and determined the significance of the individual items you have accumulated, study your clue sheet and the one above and try to figure out what it all adds up to. String together all the evidence and make a *composite* of the story and characters. This will give you a map for later when you must begin a more detailed examination of the action of the play. See if you can put what you have learned into a few paragraphs that will get to the essence of who Star and Bete are, and of the action contained in the excerpt as you understand it. When you have finished, compare your composite to the one that follows:

> Star and Bete are longtime friends and actresses who have been in the business for quite a while. They struggled together in their early days as professionals, but Star, the less talented of the two, is the one who has found the greater success, as her recent Academy Award attests. Bete feels betrayed and abandoned by her old friend and has set up this meeting so she can finally tell her egomaniac friend off. She is fueled by jealousy as much as

feelings of betrayal in that her own life choices—marriage to a drunk, having a child whom she adores—have kept her from achieving the success she feels belongs to her more than her friend. Star in turn, though enjoying the greater acclaim, argues that the success game is less attractive than the jealous Bete seems to think. In fact, she may be equally jealous of Bete's talent and tenacity, as well as some of the things that Bete has found in her life that she has sacrificed or abandoned for success. Nonetheless, by the end of the cutting, there are indications that these two old friends still love and root for each other, and their differences may be less important than their affection.

Bete has chosen the expensive and high-profile Russian Tea Room for their meeting in spite of the fact that she cannot really afford to do so. Her choice is significant, though in the excerpt we do not get the whole picture. The fact that the author points out that both actors are thirty or over also gives us relevant information regarding the stakes that help generate the conflict and action of the play. Significant also are the facts that Bete has a child she adores and a husband who, though self-destructive and unreliable, is a higher profile actor than she. The fact that Bete is auditioning for denture commercials also establishes that the biological clock is ticking for her, and perhaps helps fuel her jealousy.

· How does your analysis compare to the one above? If yours is far different from mine, re-examine the list above and your own, and see if you missed anything important that would bring you closer to the composite I have created. Remember, the point is to use specifics from the script to draw conclusions about the story and characters.

Everything stated in the description above is drawn from those specifics—whether found in the dialogue or in the action. The trick is to examine everything that is said and done, and figure out what it all adds up to. Each word and action a playwright provides means something; otherwise it wouldn't be there. The detective work is your responsibility, because you are the one who will have to tell the story on stage, moment by moment, with all the clarity and punch you can give it.

Now that you've examined the script in detail, you can use what you've learned about the situation, the characters, and their interaction to tell the playwright's story, moment by moment. It is always essential to keep in mind that a story consists of characters performing actions in a sequence. A story has a beginning, middle, and end with a central conflict or conflicts that will ensure that the journey from beginning to end is an interesting one. The characters who go on this journey will be different at the end than they were at the beginning, because the journey they go on somehow changes them. This is apparent even in the cutting that appears above. As new information is revealed, our perceptions change, even as the characters' perceptions of one another evolve. The sequence of actions that the character undertakes and/or undergoes is called the character's arc or throughline.

A story, if told correctly, also produces a desired effect on its audience. It will be helpful if you know what that effect might be. What do you think the audience should be feeling by the end of the cutting above? How do you know this? The story will most likely also have a point that becomes clear as a result of the good telling. This point is often referred to as the story's spine, and all the elements of the story should work to support that spine. Does there seem to be a point already being established to the story unfolding above? What do you think the audience should be thinking about by the end of the excerpt? Is there an issue that the play seems to be presenting for consideration? Does the playwright seem to have an attitude about that issue? Why do you think so? Knowing what this issue is and what the author is saying about it will help you make choices later on when you are called upon to do so. A story also has a tone or mood that will help make it work effectively. What is the tone of the story above? Serious, comedic? A combination? Obviously, the excerpt above is serious. It deals with serious issues and large feelings. But there is also some humor. It will be important for you to know when and where the scene is supposed to be funny in order for you to help produce the desired effects.

◇◇◇◇◇◇◇◇◇◇◇◇◇◇◇◇

With all this in mind, could you take me on the journey of the story cutting above? By focusing on the action of the story, could you relate it in a step-by-step, chronological way? It is very important that you be able to do this. In the next chapter, we'll examine the step-by step action of *Ten-Dollar Drinks* more closely, and then take a look at how finding the conflict in a play can help you make choices that will serve the script as well as the character you are portraying.

<><><><><><><><><><><><><><><><><><><><><><><><><><><><><><><><>

CHAPTER 5

Finding the Story through Conflict and Objectives

I n the last chapter, we began our detective work by examining the script as any self-respecting detective would. We pored over the script with our magnifying glasses and assembled a list of the significant clues we found there. From those telling details of the dialogue and action, we assembled a descriptive composite of the story we uncovered. This close work allowed us to begin thinking of the story as a journey with an arc that we could trace as it unfolded—even though, with only an excerpt to work with, we couldn't plot the entire course. Within the cutting we analyzed, we could still see how the characters, through a series of physical and psychological actions, pursued a throughline that would leave them different at the end of the story than they were at the beginning.

Now, as we continue our examination, let's take a closer look at the actions contained in the story. We need to identify all the gears in the Swiss watch that the playwright has painstakingly constructed. Further, we must determine how they all work together. Once we have done this, the script will become our railroad tracks of cause-and-effect actions that as actors we can follow to storytelling success. But we must also learn to stay on the tracks the playwright provides. And the railroad tracks of a script are not as visible as the railroad tracks we travel on in life, so you will have to develop your ability to see them—by using craft.

With all this in mind, this is the order of business we will follow in Chapters Five and Six:

- Map out the cause-and-effect sequence of the actions found in the play. (Once we have done so, we will have a better view of those railroad tracks mentioned above.)
- Determine the conflict in the story and discover its relationship to playing objectives.
- Analyze the action for objectives and tactics to play.
- Apply those chosen objectives and tactics to the script.
- Divide the scene into beats, using those objectives and tactics.
- Make a detailed score of the script.

Ultimately, this process will move you down the tracks of great storytelling—storytelling that is believable, compelling, and effectively serves the script. In addition, you will be playing actions that reveal who your characters are through the actions you have chosen to execute and play out.

But first, here is the play again, this time in its entirety.

◇◇◇

TEN-DOLLAR DRINKS

Characters:
STAR—thirty or over
BETE—thirty or over

Star is extremely well dressed, Bete, less so.

Setting:
A drinks table at the Russian Tea Room.

STAR   I mean *everyone* was there. Everyone.

BETE   The only stars I give a damn about are the ones on my kid's report card.

STAR   How is he...uh...

BETE   You forgot his name.

STAR   Jesse.

BETE   You forgot before you remembered. Just the way you saw me that night at Allison's, and lousy actress that you are you screwed up pretending not to see me.

STAR   I saw you at Allison's.

BETE   You are the worst.

STAR   I was surrounded by twenty sycophantic moving mouths.

BETE   Congratulations! Congratulations! But meantime we waited on your leash for you to say hi...

STAR   I had another party to go to.

BETE   We figured as much my dear, but we refused to suffer the ignominy of you leaving first and waving us a pathetic *"Dear, what can I do?"*

STAR   Talk about your son. That calms you.

BETE   He got into Trinity.

STAR   I presume that's good news.

BETE   In my world it is.

STAR   Well, that's nice.

BETE   Till my money runs out. And don't you interpret that as I got you here to ask for a handout.

STAR   Thanks. Here's to Jesse.

BETE   That I'll drink to.

STAR   Why'd you pick a place where the drinks are ten bucks?

BETE   Me, invite a star to a no-class joint?

STAR   I'll pick up the check if you let me.

BETE   You bet your sweet ass I'll let you.

STAR   What about all that voice-over work?

BETE   New producer, new voice. Yesterday I got a call for a denture spot.

STAR   You didn't.

BETE   Old people are getting younger every day, honey.

STAR   In L.A. they said you're up for that Pinter thing.

BETE   Yeah.

STAR   Tired?

BETE   Just pissed. At my husband for being a drunk, my parents for dying, the dying was bad enough but leaving me shit...

STAR   Uh.... What the hell time is it?

BETE   Now tell me you've got to go.

STAR   No, go on...your husband?

BETE   I went and fell in love with an actor who hates himself, what else is new, except this one's a drunk so I go ahead and have his kid.

STAR   You're talkin' about your son now.

BETE   A terrific kid, knock wood.

STAR   Does he see his dad?

BETE   From a cab a couple weeks ago we saw him in rotted jogging shoes with glassy eyes, walking his dog.

STAR   I thought he got himself a soap.

BETE He's on the "World" thing or "The Bold and the Broken."

STAR Then he should help with Jesse.

BETE He sends some money. (STAR *stares as if to ask,* "*Then why kvetch?*")

STAR I hate to say this, but I got a damn P.R. meeting. So...what is it? I showed up. So?

BETE Okay. I'm not jealous of you.

STAR That's it?

BETE Before we drift apart, as we obviously will, and you decide you don't know me at all anymore, I want it in the record that I'll never envy you no matter what you accumulate, acquire...

STAR You've got too much on the ball to envy anybody.

BETE True.

STAR Too bad the rest of the world hasn't acknowledged this.

BETE That's okay...(*The insult catches up to her.*) Let's keep it between you and me, shall we? (*Now letting it show.*) I'm not ashamed to look you in the eye and show you the hurt I feel.

STAR Hurt for yourself or me?

BETE Hurt that you walk around this town like you never knew a lot of your old friends.

STAR Oh, Jesus.

BETE Oh, Jesus, huh?

STAR I win that cursed thing and suddenly I need four telephones and still I have to hire someone around the apartment to screen my callers. I hear from high-school friends, relatives I never met. I'm a freak. I'm worn out...

BETE   We acted in the same company for ten years. We
ate more dinners, spent more rotten hours together. I
paid for more coffees. We slept together more nights...

STAR   You're not going around claiming that.

BETE   You dog. I meant I had to put you to sleep, you
drunk, on my couch a half dozen times. I'm not
claiming to be your sister or some high-school jerk. You
always were using everyone, everything. And it worked.
What are you complaining about? So here's to your
fucking obese ego, your obscene Oscar and your fame.
(STAR *pushes her drink away.*)

STAR   You know, what fame is? Multiply all the people
you don't wanna know by two hundred million. That's
fame. Fame...is the drink that comes to your table
from that dark corner of the restaurant and it could be
from either a deranged stalker or your future lover.
Either way if you don't drink the shit they'll hate you
till they die. There is nothing spiritual about fame.
Fame is prostitution without body contact. I know only
one person who believed she was a true goddess. She
refused to go to the bathroom because it would destroy
her status and she wound up exploding in a Los Angeles
emergency room. That's fame, honey.

BETE   Well it didn't look that way at the Academy
Awards.

STAR   (*With fear of the jealousy and the punishment.*) Did
you watch?

BETE   You looked great. You said exactly the right thing.
I was proud.

STAR   But did you watch?

BETE   Well, of course I watched.

STAR   Katie and Bill didn't watch. It's amazing how many didn't bother.

BETE   I can't believe Katie didn't watch it.

STAR   They had a gallery opening.

BETE   She saw it on the news, didn't she?

STAR   They saw nothing.

BETE   She didn't see the *paper*?

STAR   She said it wasn't delivered that day.

BETE   That bitch.

STAR   Well, nobody expected I'd get it, least of all me.

BETE   *I* didn't expect you to *get* it. You were up there with ancient deities, for heaven's sake.

STAR   Cut the bullshit.

BETE   Why? It's never for us to judge this stuff. So maybe you didn't deserve it...

STAR   I didn't say I didn't deserve it. Oh you...

BETE   I just hate you for going off into the sunset like some Wagnerian myth.

STAR   You're a better actress than I.

BETE   Just not as lucky as you. Is that the message?

STAR   You know you never were my best friend, for cryin' out loud.

BETE   But so unknown I deserved to be snubbed? You want me to buy that you don't know me at all? Ask me. I'll pretend we never met. Oh, you should be punished. God...

STAR   Oh, c'mon. Hey.

BETE   It's like watching a ship sailing away forever.

STAR   For me it's like being *on* the ship.

BETE   I never had so close a friend win one of those horrid things.

STAR Why don't you stop wasting time and tell me to
my face that you're jealous of me.

BETE What? I would despise myself if I felt one ounce
of…of jealousy of you of all people. I'm a damned
good actress, better than most of the clowns out there.

STAR Including me.

BETE Yes, and you said it yourself. And I'd hate myself if
I stooped to…to…jealousy…or…

STAR Then you hate yourself.

BETE You sonofabitch. I don't hate myself for having
my son, for…for…

STAR Your son has nothing to do with this.

BETE I couldn't drag my ass around La-La Land with
that kid.

STAR I didn't make it in L.A. I made it here on the same
stage, in the same company as you.

BETE (*Ping pong.*) I waited on tables. You've been
subsidized since you were born.

STAR I worked my ass off.

BETE You're still not good enough.

STAR So why don't you throw your drink in my face?
You've been dying to since you walked in here.

BETE Ach…throw my *drink?*

STAR Your hand's been shaking. You can hardly hold it
back. Go ahead. Someone may take a picture. You'll get
in the papers. People will gossip about it. You'll be
welded to me for life. Maybe it'll get you a part in
something.

BETE You weirdo.

STAR Oh, cut the shit. You're just as fucking hard-
hearted an entrepreneur as I am. For a month you've

72

been trying to provoke this argument. I'm here. I showed up. So go prove to the world you're intimate with a star...

BETE   You know what a star is? You piece of shit? A star is one of those gorgeous goddamn glittering things in the heavens that mankind has been staring at for millions of years. It's a fucking *sun*, a giant, burning, eternal glory that gives more life than all our little fat heads put together cannot imagine. The kind of star you are is the paper kind, with glue on the back, the kind you buy by the hundreds in a little box for a buck.

STAR   Cut the monologue and throw the *fuckin'* drink in my face. (BETE *stands in horror.*)

BETE   I'm getting out of here, you crazy sonofabitch.

STAR   Sure, because I'm wise to you. You aren't jealous, merely jealous. You're the same predatory opportunist you always were. You played your last card to get me here and you won. I'm bending to you, paying my dues so you can cut yourself in for your share of the pie. Well, take your share. Throw the goddamn drink. Throw the glass. (BETE *lifts her drink and flings it into* STAR's *face. The two continue to look at one another.* BETE *starts to leave.*) Come back. Sit. Sit down. (BETE *sits slowly, totally emptied of feeling.* STAR *grabs her hand and puts it to her cheek. She kisses* BETE's *hand gratefully, as* BETE *looks on, amazed and stunned.*)

◇◇

Every moment in the play you've just read contains a little story consisting of an action and reaction—and each of those moments follows from the previous one with the logic of cause and effect. As an actor you must show these moments of cause and effect as clearly as possible in order to tell the most compelling story. This means you must always play actions. If you play emotions instead of actions, you are far less likely to communicate that story clearly.

Remember, actions are controllable and repeatable. They are also tangible. Even emotions, by the way, no matter how deeply felt, are communicated to others more through their accompanying actions than by any direct communication of the emotions themselves. Here in an example. You just got good news that makes you very happy. You grab the pillow from your bed and hug it to you as you begin to spin yourself in a circle. It is the action and the manner in which you perform it that communicate your joy. As an actor, if you rely on emotion to tell your story, you may be heartfelt and believable, compellingly so, even, but there is no guarantee that you will be communicating your feelings to an audience, or to the actor you are working with, for that matter. Far better to focus on your actions. Emotions always follow a set of well-executed actions, by the way. Hug that pillow with commitment, and that feeling of joy is very likely to follow.

So it is your job to discover the actions and play them. The action in a story is like a set of dominoes the playwright has lined up, waiting for them to be knocked over. Once the story is set in motion, one action leads relentlessly to another through a cause-and-effect dynamic that any actor can ride. It is your job, however, to identify each action the playwright has provided you, and then to clearly execute that action when you are putting the scene or play on its feet. Once you have identified these action moments in your analysis, you will be able to shape them clearly and fully in the rehearsal part of your process.

Take a few moments now and see if you can map out the actions in *Ten-Dollar Drinks*, event by event. Finding the step-by-step action is harder than you might think. The play does not consist a lot of physical action—the things that the characters physically do. But there is a lot of psychological action—what the characters do through what they say and how they say it. The characters in *Ten-Dollar Drinks* do a lot to each other, but most of it must be translated from what is said.

Jot down your chronological list of all the things that happen, noting where possible how each event triggers the next. It may be easier to see this cause-and-effect relationship if you start at the end of the scene and work backwards to the beginning. It is always easier to retrace your steps from the end of a maze than it is to get there. You are likely to find this to be the case with charting the action of a play as well.

Once you have finished your chart, you will better understand the progression of action and how all the pieces work together, as they do in a musical score that lays out the music as it should unfold. Your score might look something like this.

> At the opening of the play, we find Bete and Star mid-conversation in an expensive New York restaurant, the Russian Tea Room. Star is describing for Bete a party she attended, noting that "everyone" (i.e., all the stars) was there. Bete undercuts Star by punning on the fact that the only stars important to her are the ones her son gets for his work in school. When Star stumbles on Bete's son's name, Bete jumps on her and compares the slight to when Star failed to introduce her friends at another party. Star admits to the snub but tries to justify it, and quickly switches back to Bete's son, a safer subject. Bete brags about her son, but this leads the conversation to the subject of her financial struggles. Star asks why, if there is money trouble, Bete has picked this expensive place for drinks. Bete and Star fire verbal barbs and Star offers to buy the drinks, to which

Bete quickly agrees as though she sees it as Star's obligation. Star changes the subject to Bete's voice-over work, which leads to Bete's confession that she was called in for a denture commercial, and Bete and Star joust a bit verbally. Star asks about Bete's possible upcoming role in a Pinter play, which leads Bete into the subject of her lousy life—little money; no help from her parents, who have died; and an alcoholic husband who is an unreliable father. Star suddenly realizes that she is late for another appointment, but Bete shames her into staying.

Then Star returns to the subject of Bete's husband and child. Bete offers up more details about her husband's soap career and drinking. Bete realizes she has been complaining, and Star uses this as an opportunity to announce that she must leave immediately for a P.R. meeting. She then asks outright why Bete has called her here. Bete responds by declaring that she is not jealous of Star. Star seems to accept this and admits that Bete is more talented. This empowers Bete to accuse Star of abandoning her old friends. Star justifies herself by explaining the difficulties of fame, and that everyone wants "a piece of her." Bete then guilts Star out by referring in detail to their shared past. Star defends herself with a speech about what a person has to give up to be famous and how hard that is. Bete counters that it didn't look so hard at the Academy Awards. Star admits to feeling pride in receiving the award. Bete admits she felt pride as well, and they bond over this shared feeling.

Bete and Star join forces to rail on other friends who chose not to share in Star's triumph. They then discuss whether Star actually deserved to win and agree that she was lucky considering the field. Star admits that Bete is the better actor. Bete admits to not being as lucky. Star informs Bete that they were never best friends. Bete counters that that fact does not justify the snubbing. She then admits to feeling left behind. Star accuses Bete of either being jealous or hating herself. Bete uses her son as an excuse for not succeeding. Star and Bete argue about who worked harder and who had the bigger obstacles to overcome. In anger Bete declares that Star is "still not good enough." Star acknowledges the anger by telling Bete to throw her drink in Star's face. Bete considers doing it, but hesitates. Star instigates further by accusing Bete of being just like her. Bete trashes the whole concept of being a star. Star finally undercuts Bete by saying, "Just throw the fucking drink in my face." Then she accuses Bete of being crazy. She provokes Bete further by returning to the jealousy theme, then tells Bete that Bete got what she wanted—a moment to be seen with a star. This finally provokes Bete into throwing the drink. They stare at each other, and finally Bete starts to leave.

Star calls after her and tells Bete to sit down. Bete slowly returns, and Star takes Bete's hand and puts it to her cheek. Then she kisses Bete's hand (gratefully, according to the stage directions). Bete looks back at Star (stunned, according to the stage directions).

Whether your score looks exactly like mine or not, if you did a careful read and truly listed all the cause-and-effect actions that you could find, you now have at least two things you did not have before: 1) a clear, moment-by-moment map of the story; and 2) an actual diagram of its mechanics. The actions of the characters are now laid out in a logical progression. The story flow that is now apparent will give you many specifics to play with when you begin your actual rehearsal of the scene.

Take a moment now and reread the score printed above. Pay particular attention to the use of verbs. You may want to jot down the verbs that particularly strike you. They will become useful later.

You might also jot down the verbs that fail to impact you. They will be far less useful. We will discuss these lists later on. In addition, when you go back over your score, see if you can determine why I split the score into paragraphs the way I did. (Hint: the answer has to do with major transitions in the actions and where they occur.) Read on after you have done the work.

Did you notice how many active verbs I used—verbs that clearly define the action of the story? This not a coincidence, of course, because verbs *are* actions. See if your own score is likewise filled with action verbs. If it isn't, you probably did not focus enough on action, and got caught up in description. You cannot play an adjective; you cannot act a description. Make verbs your friends, and use them as much as possible. Develop your ability to recognize and play actions, as many as you can, whenever you can. They will do your acting for you. This is a promise. This is one of the few axioms in the craft of acting.

Consider as an example the two stage directions at the end of the play. I'm talking about the moment when Star takes Bete's hand and puts it to her face and kisses it. These are probably the most powerful and telling actions in the entire play. And the moment has no accompanying dialogue. Nevertheless, we know more about Star's thinking and feeling at that moment than at any other time in the play. It is also incredibly moving. Nothing I could say could convince you more powerfully that your physical actions are every bit as important as what you say in terms of effective storytelling.

Some acting teachers, by the way, will advise you to ignore stage directions. I think that is misguided advice. It comes from the fact that when you read a script by Samuel French or Dramatists Play Service, the stage directions often include the original stage manager's blocking notes. These notes are intended to help amateurs find and understand the story moment by moment. They often include feelings as well as actions, and they are not always a reflection of the playwright's actual thoughts. You are never obligated to do the stage directions in a script, whether it is from an acting version or not, but you should never dismiss them before you see what they have to offer. In the case of the stage directions I mentioned above, they are Joe Pintauro's, and obviously reflect his thoughts about the action of the story, besides helping to create its most powerful moment. So don't dismiss stage directions out of hand.

Now we're ready to look at our score in terms of conflict and objectives. Without conflict there is no drama. Therefore, it is always your job as an actor to find the conflict and use it, or, if there isn't much conflict present, to create it. That, of course, won't be necessary with *Ten-Dollar Drinks*. There is plenty of conflict throughout this play. The action scores we have already created describe a lot of tension and many of the little battles that move the story forward. But as actors, we also need to identify the central issue between the characters in a play overall, and in a scene specifically—because they lead us to an overall purpose to our behavior, and keep us on the railroad tracks of the story. In addition, we will need to identify the overall objective (sometimes known as superobjective) that each of these characters is pursuing.

Take a moment now and define the conflict in this play as you see it, and then try to determine what Bete and Star really want or need as a result of their meeting in the Russian Tea Room. Why are they here? Why have they agreed to this meeting? What they want and need from each other are their respective objectives. Even if you decide that Bete and Star don't realize what they truly want from each other, as an actor you need to know those hidden objectives, so that you can tell the full story of the play through your actions. When you have determined the central conflict of the play, and each character's main objective, write your answers down. It's not enough to have a general idea in your mind. Commit to a clear intention that you've made tangible on the page, or you will never be able to use what you come up with effectively. Read on when you have finished.

Keep in mind that the work you just did is not mathematics or physics. There is no single set of right or wrong answers. But there are answers that work. If the choices you ultimately make help clarify the story and make it compelling, then you have come up with a good set of answers. If what you come up with gets in your way, or confuses or diminishes the story, then your answers are not effective ones and you must go back to the drawing board. Remember, your objectives are actions you must actually be able to play at all times. If you pick an objective and then can't play it or don't play it, get rid of it. Your job is to find actions that you actually can do *to* or *with* the other character or characters in the scene—at every moment.

Now let's review for a moment the kinds of conflicts available to playwrights and actors, because you will need to think about that. As we know, the most common and most useful conflict for actors is the person-versus-person variety—because most scenes are written that way. Two people on stage—seek the conflict between them. But the characters in *Ten-Dollar Drinks* have internal conflicts as well. Star may feel she doesn't deserve the success she has attained, for instance, and Bete may wonder how her life choices have affected her ability to succeed in the world of show business. Because life is not fair, Star has achieved the success that the more talented Bete thinks should have been hers. This has clearly compromised their friendship.

So here's how I would lay out the central conflict and the characters' primary objectives: The conflict between Bete and Star results from Star's success and Bete's relative failure in show business. This has put a great divide between these former good friends. Bete can't blame Star for her own life choices, but she can blame Star for abandoning her. Since Bete has called this meeting, I think her objective is *to make Star feel guilty* in the hope that they can regain their old friendship.

Star, who knows that Bete is the more talented actor, wants *to make Bete accept her success* so that they can still be friends.

What you think may be different. That is fine, as long as your choices are consistent with the railroad tracks of the play and give you specifics that will work for you. You may have said, for instance, that both characters simply want to find a way to become friends again. Simpler than mine, right? Sounds good, but that may become problematic because so much of the play consists of doing and saying things to each other that will keep the characters from reaching that goal. When actors play actions or tactics that don't get them toward what they want, we say they are making *negative choices*.

You should never play a negative choice. A negative choice seldom moves the action forward, and is likely to confuse the action the playwright has provided. It often becomes static or boring as well. So avoid negative choices. If that means changing or modifying your objective or tactics, so be it. Remember, you must always make choices that move you toward your overall objective. Yes, the new information and discoveries the playwright gives you can provide obstacles to overcome. And victories and defeats along the way can lead you to new objectives and tactics to employ. And yes again, your objectives can change during the course of a play or scene. But—as an actor playing a character—you must have a strong and specific objective to play as the scene begins, and you must actually be able to play it. Star has agreed to meet with Bete for a reason. And you as the actor making the choices must know that reason, even when your character doesn't. So finding an objective you can stick with by altering your tactics should always be your desired goal. Stating an objective and then not playing it simply will not serve you or the play.

Remember—playing objectives and tactics specifically and at all times will keep you on the railroad track that the playwright has provided. This can be especially challenging when the central conflict is masked because the characters don't deal with each other directly and avoid exposing what is really going on. In those situations, we must find the subtext in the dialogue (what the characters really mean when they are saying something else). But that is clearly not the case in *Ten-Dollar Drinks*. Here the characters mostly say exactly what they mean, and say it clearly, because they need or want something very badly. The stakes are incredibly high—the survival of a long-term friendship. And the urgency is equally so—who knows how much time Star is willing to spend with an estranged friend from her past?

So let's assume that my stated objectives for these characters are workable. Go back and reread the play focusing on Bete and Star's objectives. As you read, ask yourself whether the action of the play in terms of dialogue and anything physical that occurs is consistent with those stated objectives. Continue reading after you have reassessed the play.

Assuming you have reread *Ten-Dollar Drinks*, here are some questions about your reading. Can everything the characters say and do be justified in accordance with the overall objectives we laid out? Do their tactics make logical sense when you consider them in terms of their overall objectives? Do the verbs that we noted earlier become clear tactics as you reread—now that you see those tactics in terms of the characters' overall objectives? If the answers to these questions are in the affirmative, then you have overall objectives that should serve you well.

Now it's time to take a closer look at the tactics that you as the actor playing one of these characters might employ in pursuit of her objective. If you go back and examine the cause-and-effect action score that I wrote above, you will probably find that many of the verbs I used will convert easily into tactics. Others, even in the list of strong verbs you noted, may not be useful as a tactic or may be a weaker version of a stronger and more specific action that should be played.

Here is a list of verbs from the first paragraph of our cause-and-effect score. Take a few moments and examine them carefully. Do these verbs represent solid tactics that can be played clearly and compellingly? Do they make for positive choices? Do they tactically move the characters closer to their objectives? Do these verbs represent actions that can be landed on the other character? Which verbs need to be replaced? Which verbs should be altered to turn them into the best tactics possible? Make any changes you feel are necessary to these verbs. Remember: strong transitive verbs—verbs that give you very specific actions to play, actions that do something to the other character—are the best kinds of verbs to use and to play. The stronger and more specific, the better. Read on only after you have done the work.

Star is describing	Star offers
Bete undercuts	Bete quickly agrees
Bete jumps on her and compares	Star changes the subject
Star admits	Bete's confession
Star tries to justify	Star asks
Bete brags	Star suddenly realizes
Star asks	Bete shames

Again, there are no absolutes here, no mathematical "This is correct; that is not." A particular verb, whether I think it is weak or not, might trigger a strong and specific action in you. All that being said, in general, the more specific and urgent you can be in your analysis choices, the more likely it is that your actual work later in the rehearsal process will be equally so. With that caveat in mind, here follows some hopefully useful commentary on the verbs listed above.

The first action, "Star is describing," is immediately weakened by the use of the verb "to be" (in the form of "is"). You can never play a state of being. It is not an action by definition. But even when we change it to an action verb, "Star describes," tactically it still has no power to affect Bete. So, if you come up with such a verb, ask yourself what is really going on in the moment being described. A closer look at the score and you will see that Star is describing a party she attended and she is trying to *impress* Bete with the fact that several stars were in attendance. That is a tactic that you could play—one that will impact Bete and take Star closer to her desired objective. Impressing Bete may work toward getting her on board with Star's success—you know me and I know them and if we're friends, maybe you can know them, too. Notice the practical logic in this choice.

The next action listed, "Bete undercuts," is a strong action verb that conjures up a mental picture of a physical act. That easily transfers into a strong action to play—one that would clearly have an effect on Star. This is a good actor's verb to use as a tactic.

"Bete jumps on her and compares," the next deliberate actions, are of course two distinct actions combined into a summary of events from the score. "Bete jumps on" is the stronger of the two, because, even used as a metaphor, it conjures up the image of a strong physical action. "Compares" is less useful, a neutral description of a piece of dialogue. A stronger action verb that would be tactical might be something like "Bete puts down the manner in which Star behaved" or "Bete criticizes Star's bad behavior." Perhaps you can come up with a stronger phrase, but hopefully you're beginning to follow the logic and the usefulness of finding good action verbs to play.

The next verb, "to admit," comes with a tactical implication built in. Whenever we admit something, we are agreeing to give power to the person we are admitting to, and it is usually something difficult to do. Therefore something is automatically at stake, which makes it interesting. Tactically, when you admit something it is a voluntary loss. When you as an actor choose to admit something as your character, you are changing the dynamic between you and the person you are in conflict with. You are making a good chess move. Again, Star is working toward her objective through the use of tactics.

"To justify" is also a verb that represents a solid action to play. And tactically it is a good action to follow an action like "to admit." Admitting makes one vulnerable, but justifying something you did gives you the opportunity to take back some of the power you gave up a moment ago. In the cause-and-effect sequence of actions, and in a chess game you want to win, it seems like a good tactical move to make in reclaiming the road toward the victory of achieving your objective.

"Bete brags" is a strong action. It is specific and definitely provides an actor with something to do. But tactically it seems like a negative choice. No one is drawn to someone who brags. Bete does brag in that moment, but the moment is not really about the bragging. Tactically Bete is trying *to make Star feel bad* for her life choices that have denied her the opportunity to have a life outside her career. Bragging, by nature, is about the person bragging, not about the person whom you are trying to affect. So in this situation, bragging, though a strong verb, is probably not the right action to play. However, the use of the phrase "to make someone _____" is always a good, strong way to create an action that will land.

The next listed verb phrase, "Star asks," is extremely weak in terms of specificity and tactical power. By virtue of asking, it's over and done with, and what has the asking in and of itself accomplished? If you go back to this moment, what Star is really doing here is challenging Bete on her choice to come to the Russian Tea Room when she has no money. "To challenge" is a strong verb that lands on the receiver powerfully and is a solid tactic as well. Why not use it?

What do you think of the next action, "Star offers"? Again, an offer is a suggestion to give something, and to give something is always a good tactical move. This verb is playable and useful. How about "Bete quickly agrees"? Follow the kind of logic previously employed and decide whether "agreeing" is a good tactic at this point in the action. Be sure to justify your answer specifically and clearly.

"Star changes the subject" is a good tactical move for her at the moment in the play where she does so, but tactically it only lasts a moment. Remember, as actors playing characters, you must be playing your objective, or tactics to achieve your objective, at all times. So Star is changing the subject—an action that is over very quickly—with a new tactic in mind. And you as the actor need to think about what that new tactic is. Again, the character may not be aware of this, but the actor playing the character must operate with an understanding of the forward progression of the story at all times. This is a major difference between acting and real life.

Of the verb phrases remaining, "Bete shames" is probably the strongest. Can you figure out why? "Star asks" should be changed to another verb because it is of little use tactically. "Bete's confession" needs to be changed to "Bete confesses" for reasons that are obvious by now, right? But you still must ask yourself whether confessing is a good tactic. (It probably is.) And finally, Star may "suddenly realize," but how does that work tactically? Could it be another transitional moment of discovery that must immediately segue into another set of tactics to play? You'd better believe it.

Again, there are no absolute answers in this process; there are only answers that work best to obtain the overall objectives of the actors as characters, and to tell the story of the play and your character effectively. Both of the characters in this play have internal conflicts that will add obstacles to achieving their goals and that will help create high risk and urgency as they play out their tactics to move toward their objectives.

At this point I suggest you go through the entire action score and examine all the verbs used there. Make any changes necessary as we did for the first paragraph of the score above. If my description proves vague in spots, don't hesitate to reference the actual script and make adjustments where you think they need to be made. If you then go through the entire script, and I strongly suggest that you do, you will discover that you now have a detailed set of tactics that can actually be played. In the next chapter, we will discover how to translate those tactics to the stage.

CHAPTER SIX

◇◇◇◇◇◇◇◇◇◇◇◇◇◇◇◇◇◇◇◇◇◇◇◇◇◇◇◇◇◇◇◇◇

Taking Control
of the Script

In the last chapter we examined the close relationship between conflict
and objectives, and broke the play *Ten-Dollar Drinks* into a series of
cause-and-effect actions. By examining the verbs used in our action
score, we were able to identify many of the tactics used by the characters
in pursuit of those objectives. With that information in hand, we could
see the play in terms of its tactical progression. We were able to trace the
trail of tactics, and noted where one ended and another took its place.

In this chapter we will take the work we did in Chapter Five and
apply it directly to the script. By the time we are finished, you will
have an in-hand map representing the moment-to-moment work you
must do during the course of the play. You will have a guidebook
showing you what your job is as an actor at every moment you are
on stage. Never again should you feel like those freshman actors
mentioned in the introduction—the ones who didn't have a clue
what to do when a script was first put in their hands.

Before we go on, let's take a few moments now to review the most
important concepts we worked with in the last chapter.

We began with conflict, the engine of drama, the cornerstone of
storytelling, the heart of action-based acting. Talking about conflict

automatically led us to a discussion of objective—the prize an actor as character must pursue at all times. Unlike in life, where people often do things without realizing why they do them, you learned that, as an actor, you must make choices for your character even when your character may not consciously be doing so. You found specific objectives to pursue, and tactics to achieve those objectives. You learned about making effective choices and committing to them. You learned to avoid actions that do not contribute to the story. In conclusion, then, you learned that by pursuing strong and clear objectives at all times, you will be fulfilling the obligations laid out by the script.

Now let's look at how you as an actor will play those objectives and tactics. How will you translate the psychological actions we identified in *Ten-Dollar Drinks* into physical actions that convey character and tell the story of the play? Though Star and Bete are sitting at a table, there are still some very important physical actions related to their objectives that can and must be employed. For instance, when Star suggests that she is about to leave ("Uh...what the hell time is it?"), does she start to get up? If she does, might Bete physically do something to try to stop her? Might she put a hand on Star's wrist as she starts to rise? How would she do so? Gently? With force or authority? Or might she start to stand up at the same time? What kind of eye contact are the actors as characters engaging in at that moment? Not all of these kinds of physical actions need to be planned out in advance. Many will be discovered in rehearsal. But if in your analysis work you develop an understanding of what might happen, you will have something to work with, something to bring to the table. That is always an advantage. It is always easier to create something from something than something from nothing.

There will also be business going on while sitting at the table. When do the characters drink, for instance? How do they drink? What do they drink? Do they take sips and put their glasses down?

Do they keep their glasses in hand? Which are better choices? What do these choices tell us about the characters? When do they look around? When do they look at each other? When do they look away from each other? How do they execute each of the things they physically do? What you do, how you do it, when you do it—all of it impacts the storytelling and the way the audience perceives your character. How you execute every moment will affect the ongoing story and give the audience information regarding what you are thinking and feeling at that moment. If Star leans in toward Bete at a particular moment, it will have dramatic power. If Bete pulls away, it will have dramatic power. You must be making physical choices that are as clear and as gripping as possible at all times.

All of your actions will have beginnings, middles, and ends. This is true for movement from place to place, ongoing business, and any gestures you come up with. If the actor playing Star rises from the table, for instance, that movement begins, not with the action itself, but with the decision or impulse to do so. Whether the actor as character has thought through a decision or acted on impulse will inform and affect the manner in which she actually gets up. Further, if she can somehow demonstrate her thinking process to the audience by what she does physically, then the actor is telling the story in the best possible way. Physical actions give actors the opportunity to show what their characters are thinking and feeling at every moment.

In life, we may be unaware of why we reach for a drink when we do, why we take a bite of our dinner at a particular moment, why we cut our beef when we do, how we do it, etc. But as actors playing characters having drinks in the Russian Tea Room, we must use the impulse to drink, the actual act of drinking, and the end of the drinking action to communicate something about our characters' thinking and feeling. Star starts to rise. Bete does not reach for Star's wrist. She simply says her line, "Now tell me you have to go," without looking up. She reaches for her cocktail and, without looking at Star, she drinks. Star watches her and decides to sit down. The story of that moment is told clearly. We have a good idea about what each of the characters is thinking and feeling, and much of our idea resulted from what the actors chose to do physically, and how they completed their actions with beginnings, middles, and ends. Or perhaps it would be better for the story if Bete *looks* at Star as she drinks, and she downs all that is left in the glass deliberately while staring right into Star's eyes. She is making a point. You get the idea.

Some of the most powerful moments you will create on stage through your actions will be transitional moments—those times when the actor as character shifts from one objective or tactic to the next after experiencing a victory or defeat, or because of new information, a discovery, or an interruption. You'll recall that a *beat* is the term given to the length of script during which an actor plays a particular objective or tactic. Whenever a beat ends, for any one of the reasons just mentioned, it is the actor's job to transition from one beat to another clearly and believably. Sometimes this can be done without fanfare, but often it will be necessary for the actor as character to show how and why this change happens. What is more, these moments often occur without dialogue to explain what is going on or how the characters feel about it. So, if it is not dialogue that is going to make that information clear, then it must be what the actors choose to do physically that tells the story of those moments.

If you haven't already done so, examine the script of *Ten-Dollar Drinks* to locate all the transitional moments you can find. Read through the play in sequence so you will be sure not to miss any. Pay attention to the objectives and tactics being played and where they end. Decide whether those beats end with a victory, defeat, discovery, or new information that changes the flow of the story. Make a note in your script where each transition occurs and what the cause of the transitional moment is. Then take a few moments with each transition and try to figure out how you might physically show what each character is thinking and feeling at that particular moment. You might even try going through a series of physical actions that will make those moments clear and compelling. Be sure that each sequence has a beginning, middle, and end. Also keep in mind that these moments do not happen in a vacuum. The other character will be watching and reacting to what she sees. So you can't disregard the other actor as character when you create your transitional moment. Continue reading when you have completed your work.

At this point in our work together, you have accumulated the following useful information from all our close work on the script:

- A clearly defined conception of the story and how it progresses
- An understanding of the cause-and-effect journey of the story and the characters in that story
- A recognition of the big events that occur in the story
- A series of clearly defined objectives and tactics for each of the characters
- A recognition of where those objectives change (transitional moments)
- Some distinct ideas about possible physical actions and where they might be played

Armed with all this information, wouldn't you be wise to notate it all into your script? That way it will be available to you as you continue to prepare and develop your work. Many actors find this kind of notation extremely helpful. It will serve you much like a musical score that enables a conductor or player to do what he needs to at every moment of the work as it unfolds. If you have a system for notating all that you must do as an actor at every moment—one that is clear and accessible—it will provide you with an equally useful score. And it will be right there at your fingertips, reminding you to take care of all your necessary business.

If you choose to write directly on your script (or a photocopy of the script if the script is not yours), you will not have room for detailed explications of the things you want to keep in mind. So you are going to have to learn to make notations that are brief and to the point. If you're going to use your score as a rehearsal aid as well as a preparation guide, you will not have time to read an essay while trying to listen intently to the actors you're working with. But, with a shorthand system of notation that you understand, you'll be able to mark your script succinctly and effectively.

Below you will find directions for a system that I use with my own students. Feel free to revise and adapt it for your own purposes. Use it in the ways that serve you best. Remember, as with all the craft you are learning, you are doing so to become a better, more efficient and reliable actor. The craft you learn should be at your service, not the other way around. But don't ever discard the craft you are being offered before fully understanding how to use it properly. Once you have done that, embrace it, modify it, or ignore it. It is there to serve you. You may want to enlarge the script while you are copying it, to make it easier to read and to give you more room for your own notation. Always use a pencil for notations so that the notes you take can be changed. Your ideas about the scene *will* change as you work with a director and other actors. You will need to adjust your notations to reflect the changes in your understanding of the work and/or the needs of the production you are working on.

My Notation System

1. Write at the top of the scene your overall objective.
2. Divide the scene into beats by drawing a line across the page where each beat ends. At the top of each new beat on the left side, clearly state your new objective and/or the specific tactic you are now using.
3. On the right side of your script, write a brief explanation for each transition you make (victories, defeats, discoveries, new ideas, etc.).
4. Also use this space to briefly describe possible physical actions that would show what your character might be thinking or feeling.
5. Examine your lines. Circle or highlight any word or group of words that will be particularly useful to emphasize when you say them.
6. Examine the other characters' lines. Circle any new information (information that your character did not previously know), including stage directions hinted at through the dialogue. Remember, responding to this new information is actable.
7. Highlight or box the major dramatic moments of the scene you are doing. Double box the climax.

Now let's work through the scoring system and review the analytic techniques it references.

1. Write at the top of the scene your overall objective.

The overall objective that is listed at the beginning of a scene—or, for that matter, any specific beat objective or tactic—should contain a strong, specific verb that allows you to land that action on the other character involved in your conflict. It should be a goal that you really can attain under the circumstances. If you state an objective in terms of "to make someone do something," as in "to make Star feel horrible," it will connect you with the other actor or actors, and can be accomplished in a tangible way. If the objective serves the needs of your character and is consistent with what is happening in that section of the script, you have selected a solid objective.

Your objectives and tactics should change if they prove to be ineffective. But if you can find that overall objective that your character continues to pursue throughout the scene, it will give you a tangible railroad track to stay on. Try to find an objective that is simple, clear, and logical. If you have a problem identifying your overall objective, try looking at the scene from the outside as the audience would see it. This may give you the perspective you need to see what your character is doing. By writing the selected objective at the top of the scene, you will soon know whether it is a good one or not. If you can play what you have written there throughout the scene, if it enables you to stay on track with the logical progression of the scene, and if it is dramatically interesting, you have probably chosen an effective objective.

Objective playing may seem simplistic and not necessarily in line with how people behave in real life, but acting is not in fact like life; it just looks like it when well done. Playing objectives or tactics at all times keeps you true to the story that you are responsible for telling. The audience will add any necessary additional complexity from what they know as they watch

2. Divide the scene into beats by drawing a line across the page after each beat ends. At the top of each new beat on the left side, clearly state the new objective or tactic.

Every time you change your strategy, there is a reason for it suggested in the script. When you know a change in tactics or objective is made, mark it with a line across the page.

3. On the right side of your copy of the script, write an explanation for each transition. (It could be a discovery, a new idea, a defeat, a victory, etc.)

Remember, a *beat* is the length of script during which you pursue a particular objective or tactic. Beat changes, or *transitions*, occur when you give up on a particular objective or tactic and replace it with a new one. These changes come as a result of victories, defeats, discoveries, or interruptions. A beat might begin when Star demands that Bete throw her drink in Star's face. At the moment Bete actually does so, it is a victory for Star and a defeat for Bete. The moment after it happens is transitional, with a beginning, middle, and end. Each character takes in the moment, reacts to the moment, and then finds a new objective and/or tactic to play. What exactly goes through each character's mind during this moment is not revealed by the playwright. You only know what happens next through the dialogue and stage direction. When you make decisions about what your character is thinking and feeling, you can make some notation on the right as per the next step listed.

4. Also use this space to briefly describe subtext and psychological and physical actions that you will eventually use to make the story tangible to an audience.

It is important to remember that dialogue is only one part of your storytelling obligations. What a character says is not necessarily what she means, and what a character is thinking and feeling may not be reflected in her words. The playwright provides only the skeleton of the story in his written dialogue. Therefore it is your responsibility to fill in the rest. You will fill in many of these blank spots during the rehearsal process, but as an actor you must start thinking about your storytelling obligations during your preparation. By noting some possibilities in your initial work (in pencil, of course), you will have something to bring to rehearsal for development or until you learn something more useful and replace it later in the process.

You can also begin thinking about the ways you can use physical action to get what you need in the scene. A playwright may provide stage directions that give you some clues as to what is happening physically through the dialogue, but much of what occurs physically in the story will arise from what you and your director come up with. In a production situation, the director may provide you with some of the physical story, or may work collaboratively with you to do so; but in a scene study situation, it is up to you to provide your own blocking choices. That means you will need to think on your own about what works and what doesn't.

5. Examine your lines. Circle or highlight any word or group of words that will be particularly useful to emphasize when you say them.

Since at every moment you will be playing an objective or tactic, there are particular words and phrases that will have more force or utility in landing that tactic or getting you toward your objective. Some of these you will find in the moment during the rehearsal process. They will spontaneously come out of you as you listen and react moment by moment. But finding words and phrases and noting them in your script during your preparation will make it easier for you to get what you need from your acting partners later when you are working with them.

6. Examine the other characters' lines. Circle or highlight any new information (information that your character did not previously know), including stage directions hinted at through the dialogue. Remember, responding to this new information is actable.

Beginning actors have a tendency to not listen on stage, and listening is often the key to the best kind of acting—the kind that seems totally spontaneous and of the moment. Early in the rehearsal process you'll be distracted by trying to remember your lines and focusing on the physical actions you must execute. But once you master these obstacles, you'll get to the point when you won't have to think about this stuff any more. It will be in your muscle memory. When you reach that point you should be totally available to see and hear what is going on in the actual moment-by-moment work on stage. This is the time when you are most likely to produce surprisingly original and compelling choices that are totally believable and of the moment. By identifying as part of the homework the important information that the other characters say and do, you will be better prepared to listen for these lines and respond to them when the time comes. By marking those pieces of dialogue in your script, you will give yourself a useful visual reminder to do so.

7. Highlight or box the major dramatic moments of the scene. Double box the climax.

Remember that playwrights write scenes centered on a conflict that builds towards a climax and resolution. You have charted that build in your earlier work and isolated those money moments that are the stepping-stones in that progression. By boxing the dramatic moments that spring from the cause-and-effect sequence of action in a scene, you will be able to see right on your script where these moments are placed. You will have a visual reminder of how to build from each of these moments to the next. This arc that you create is more likely to be exciting and economical if you build your acting choices in accordance with the map that the boxing gives you.

Below you will find an example of how a portion of a scored scene might look. It is not meant to be read as the only way the scene can be broken down. It is intended only as an example of the process described above. The score is from the point of view of the actor playing Star. Feel free go back and improve on the work I have done. In fact, I strongly encourage you to do so—from beginning to end, and for both characters. The more you go through this process, the faster you will get good at it—and the sooner you will have this important tool at your fingertips.

◇◇

OBJECTIVE: To make Bete admit she is jealous

Tactic: to provoke Bete

STAR Why don't you stop wasting time and tell me to my face that you're jealous of me.

BETE What? I would despise myself if I felt one ounce of... of jealousy of you of all people. I'm a damned good actress, better than most of the clowns out there.

STAR Including me.

BETE Yes, and you said it yourself. And I'd hate myself if I stooped to... to... jealousy... or...

Star discovers that Bete is still denying that she is jealous.

Tactic: to put words in Bete's mouth

STAR Then you hate yourself.

BETE You sonofabitch. I don't hate myself for having my son, for... for...

Star interrupts Bete's objective and tactic.

Tactic: to interrupt and correct

STAR Your son has nothing to do with this.

BETE I couldn't drag my ass around La-La Land with that kid.

STAR I didn't make it in L.A. I made it here on the same stage, in the same company as you.

BETE (*Ping pong.*) I waited on tables. You've been subsidized since you were born.

STAR I worked my ass off.

BETE   You're still not good enough.

<table>
<tr><td>Tactic: to call her bluff</td><td>

STAR   So why don't you throw your drink in my face? You've been dying to since you walked in here.

</td><td>Star reacts to Bete's verbal victory.</td></tr>
</table>

BETE   Ach...throw my *drink?*

<table>
<tr><td>Tactic: to antagonize her into throwing drink</td><td>

STAR   Your hand's been shaking. You can hardly hold it back. Go ahead. Someone may take a picture. You'll get in the papers. People will gossip about it. You'll be welded to me for life. Maybe it'll get you a part in something.

</td><td>Star comes back with a stronger and nastier tactic.</td></tr>
</table>

BETE   You weirdo.

<table>
<tr><td>Tactic: to call her on her B.S. and rub her face in it</td><td>

STAR   Oh, cut the shit. You're just as fucking hard-hearted an entrepreneur as I am. For a month you've been trying to provoke this argument. I'm here. I showed up. So go prove to the world you're intimate with a star...

</td><td>Star has another victory: "weirdo" is a limp response by Bete. Star puts on more pressure.</td></tr>
</table>

BETE   You know what a star is? You piece of shit? A star is one of those gorgeous goddamn glittering things in the heavens that mankind has been staring at for millions of years. It's a fucking *sun*, a giant, burning, eternal glory that gives more life than all our little fat heads put together cannot imagine. The kind of star you are is the paper kind, with glue on the back, the kind you buy by the hundreds in a little box for a buck.

STAR   Cut the monologue and throw the *fuckin'* drink in my face. (BETE *stands in horror.*)

<table>
<tr><td></td><td>

BETE   I'm getting out of here, you crazy sonofabitch.

</td><td>Star defeats Bete again; leaving is a defensive choice by Bete. She is retreating.</td></tr>
<tr><td>Tactic: to verbally slap her into throwing drink</td><td>

STAR   Sure, because I'm wise to you. You aren't jealous, merely jealous. You're the same

</td><td></td></tr>
</table>

predatory opportunist you always were. You
played your last card to get me here and you

OBJECTIVE: to make up with Bete

won. I'm bending to you, paying my dues so
you can cut yourself in for your share of the pie.
Well, take your share. Throw the goddamn
drink. Throw the glass. (BETE *lifts her drink
and flings it into* STAR's *face. The two continue
to look at one another.* BETE *starts to leave.*)
Come back. Sit. Sit down. (BETE *sits slowly,*

Tactic: to make Bete know she loves her

totally emptied of feeling. STAR *grabs her hand
and puts it to her cheek. She kisses* BETE's *hand
gratefully, as Bete looks on, amazed and stunned.*)

Come up with a good physical reaction to Bete's throwing the drink. Could literally doing nothing be the best choice? Maybe a smile?

Now let's take a look at my score a little more closely (see images on following two pages), by going through the numerical process suggested above.

1 and 2. Notice that both of my main objectives in this section are very specific. *To make Bete admit that she is jealous* is a clearly stated ambition, and victory will also be clear, if and when Star achieves it. Bete will have to either literally say that she is jealous, or show it in a way that is irrefutable. Each of the tactics Star uses in trying to make that confession happen employs either a clear action verb—"to antagonize," for instance—or a metaphorical verb phrase that has a strong emotional charge. Since I came up with each of those phrases, as an actor I would know exactly how to deliver them. In other words, they are actions I know how to play. To "rub her face in it" or "verbally slap her" are actions that give me specific things to try out on my scene partner. Both seem like tactics that could lead to an admission.

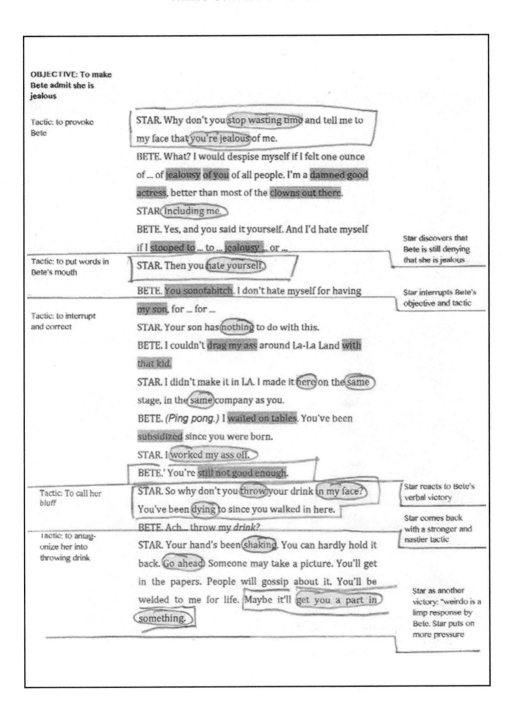

OBJECTIVE: To make Bete admit she is jealous

Tactic: to provoke Bete

STAR. Why don't you stop wasting time and tell me to my face that you're jealous of me.

BETE. What? I would despise myself if I felt one ounce of ... of jealousy of you of all people. I'm a damned good actress, better than most of the clowns out there.

STAR. Including me.

BETE. Yes, and you said it yourself. And I'd hate myself if I stooped to ... to ... jealousy ... or ...

Star discovers that Bete is still denying that she is jealous

Tactic: to put words in Bete's mouth

STAR. Then you hate yourself.

BETE. You sonofabitch. I don't hate myself for having my son, for ... for ...

Star interrupts Bete's objective and tactic

Tactic: to interrupt and correct

STAR. Your son has nothing to do with this.

BETE. I couldn't drag my ass around La-La Land with that kid.

STAR. I didn't make it in LA. I made it here on the same stage, in the same company as you.

BETE. *(Ping pong.)* I waited on tables. You've been subsidized since you were born.

STAR. I worked my ass off.

BETE.' You're still not good enough.

Tactic: To call her bluff

STAR. So why don't you throw your drink in my face? You've been dying to since you walked in here.

Star reacts to Bete's verbal victory

BETE. Ach... throw my *drink?*

Tactic: to antagonize her into throwing drink

STAR. Your hand's been shaking. You can hardly hold it back. Go ahead. Someone may take a picture. You'll get in the papers. People will gossip about it. You'll be welded to me for life. Maybe it'll get you a part in something.

Star comes back with a stronger and nastier tactic

Star as another victory: "weirdo is a limp response by Bete. Star puts on more pressure

BETE. You weirdo.

STAR. Oh, cut the shit. You're just as fucking hard-hearted an entrepreneur as I am. For a month you've been trying to provoke this argument. I'm here. I showed up. So go prove to the world you're intimate with a star ...

BETE. You know what a star is? You piece of shit? A star is one of those gorgeous goddamn glittering things in the heavens that mankind has been staring at for millions of years. It's a fucking sun, a giant, burning, eternal glory that gives more life than all our little fat heads put together cannot imagine. The kind of star you are is the paper kind, with glue on the back, the kind you buy by the hundreds in a little box for a buck.

STAR. Cut the monologue and throw the fuckin' drink in my face. *(Bete stands in horror.)*

BETE. I'm getting out of here, you crazy sonofabitch.

STAR. Sure, because I'm wise to you. You aren't jealous, merely jealous. You're the same predatory opportunist you always were~ You played your last card to get me here and you won. I'm bending to you, paying my dues so you can cut yourself in for your share of the pie. Well, take your share. Throw the goddamn drink. Throw the glass. *(Bete lifts her drink and flings it into Star's face. The two continue to look at one another. Bete starts to leave.)* Come back. Sit. Sit down. *(Bete sits slowly, totally emptied of feeling. Star grabs her hand and puts it to her cheek. She kisses Bete's hand gratefully, as Bete looks on, amazed and stunned.)*

Tactic: to call her on her B.S. and rub her face in it

Tactic: to verbally slap her into throwing drink

OBJECTIVE: to make up with Bete

Tactic: to make Bete know she loves her

Star defeats Bete again; leaving is a defensive choice by Bete. She is retreating.

Come up with a good physical reaction to Bete's throwing the drink. Could literally doing nothing be the best choice? Maybe a smile?

3. Since you probably came up with a different set of objectives and/ or tactics than I did, your beat endings are likely to be different as well. Again, that is fine. None of this is science and no two actors' choices will ever be identical, nor should they be. We all bring our individuality and our personal life experiences to the work.

But notice that in my score there is a combination of victories, losses, discoveries, and even an interruption or two. While there are no interruptions from new characters or events, Star makes some in-the-moment discoveries that quickly lead her to interrupt as a tactic.

4. I also made a few notes regarding what Star was thinking and feeling at transitional moments—notes that I could build on later. I made only one reference to Star's physical actions—at the drink-throwing moment—but I certainly could have made some other suggestions to myself at other points in the script. Perhaps you did on yours. There would certainly be more notation about physical actions had I been scoring the scene from Bete's point of view. Remember when we looked at her options in terms of gesture, ongoing business, eye contact, and movement during a single exchange with Star? You may want to go back and review that discussion to better understand how your note-taking with the score should be a shorthand for your deeper understanding of the scene.

5. When you go through the process of circling or highlighting the words and phrases that are most important to emphasize, the connection between what you say and what you do becomes very clear. The dialogue becomes a tool for attaining our objectives and succeeding with our tactics. The specific words and phrases that are the most useful to us in reaching our objectives are known as *operatives*. Clearly, the ones I circled for Star are particularly powerful and useful in her overall quest to make Bete admit to her jealousy. As tactical

weapons, these words and phrases are like little heat-seeking missiles that can be aimed right at Bete's heart. Most of the time, when skilled actors are focused on their objectives, they will automatically hit operative words and phrases, but noting what words really have such power during your analysis phase of the work can only help you up the road. Remember, craft helps you efficiently get to the point where you no longer have to think about all that you need to be doing. The faster you get to that point, the sooner you'll be able to live in the moment—where the real artistry happens.

6. Interestingly, if you read off only the portions of Bete's dialogue that I chose to highlight, you would get a sense of who she is and why she is angry. In life we do this automatically when we listen to people in conversation. Moment by moment, we record what seems important and draw conclusions from our little impressions. And we continue to modify those impressions as we get more information. As actors we need to do that as well. Noting those places in the other character's dialogue that would have an impact on us will help us later in the process when we are actually called upon to listen. Of course, you will have to adjust your initial thoughts about that dialogue in accordance with how your acting partners play those lines you noted, but again, it never hurts to have an idea of what to look for. Though I did not make any notes regarding Star's reactions to Bete's high-lighted words and phrases, you may want to do so. These notes might be in terms of your reaction internally, or they might be in terms of actual things you do physically to show what you are thinking and feeling. How, for instance, might Star react when hearing Bete say that Star is "still not good enough"? Food for thought, right?

7. Obviously, the climax of the scene is when Bete actually throws the drink in Star's face. The action builds toward this moment for quite

some time, and there are few physical actions I can think of that would be more powerful—getting on your hands and knees and begging, perhaps, or spitting in someone's face. But throwing a drink at someone is definitely a high-octane action and makes for a very satisfying climactic moment. Isolating this as the biggest moment was a fairly easy task, but the actors will have a big responsibility later in performance in living up to and surpassing what's on the page.

If you go back now and examine the other little islands of drama in the short section used for my scoring example, you will see a nice sequence of action moments that you can use for connecting the dots of the scene.

- **STAR** Why don't you stop wasting time and tell me to my face that you're jealous of me.
- **STAR** Then you hate yourself.
- **BETE** You're still not good enough.
- **STAR** So why don't you throw your drink in my face?
- **STAR** Maybe it'll get you a part in something.
- **STAR** ...you're intimate with a star...
- **BETE** You know what a star is? You piece of shit? A star is one of those gorgeous goddamn glittering things in the heavens that mankind has been staring at for millions of years. It's a fucking *sun*, a giant, burning, eternal glory that gives more life than all our little fat heads put together cannot imagine. The kind of star you are is the paper kind, with glue on the back, the kind you buy by the hundreds in a little box for a buck.
- **STAR** Cut the monologue and throw the *fuckin'* drink in my face.
- (BETE *lifts her drink and flings it into* STAR's *face. The two continue to look at one another.*)

Again, your list of stepping-stones may not match mine, but the list above does have a connect-the-dots progression that would help you map the actual story. I chose to include Bete's entire "star" speech because it is climactic in and of itself. The speech must be delivered with a passion and earnestness that will give the actor playing Bete the impetus to fling the drink at Star after Star's withering response to it. As noted previously, the flying drink speaks for itself.

In conclusion, then, like much of the scoring work we have done, selecting the major dramatic moments for boxing is a subjective process. The point is to try to find major stepping-stones in the cause-and-effect journey of the action. This will give you a clearer idea of the story you are telling because the distance between any two stones is far more manageable than having to keep in mind the entire arc of the story. Instead of needing to know the route to the entire scene by memory, you can now focus on the journey between two smaller destinations—from one event to the next until all the dots are connected. All of my choices are up for discussion, however, and it is important to remember that scoring is not about being right or wrong. It is an aid to help you find your way efficiently through the script. Clearly, you are free to interpret the script and score it in any way that will best help you to tell the playwright's story in the clearest, cleanest, most compelling way possible.

For practice, you may want to work through the analysis of this entire play for one of the characters. Better yet, do it from the point of view of each character (I would suggest doing one character at a time). Then make it a habit when you read a play that you'll be working on to do a complete analysis along the lines we've been using here, and to create a useful score. Ultimately, your goal should be to make all these basic skills as easily available to you as the act of reading has now become. Remember, you did this by practice and repetition.

When you can do this work efficiently and reliably, you will begin to realize a major payoff: that doing this kind of work honestly and completely has made you a better actor. You will find yourself producing more interesting, more exciting, and more believable work in a shorter time. In other words, you will have developed what every working actor desperately wants to possess: a technique that serves you in any scripted acting situation.

One more thought before we leave this topic. If you are not actually in a class at the moment, you may want to find a partner with whom you can work, so that you can practice all the skills involved when reading from a script that you have scored. Obviously, it is a great benefit having so many useful notes right there in front of you to work with. But it can also be a burden if you can't handle all that information readily. Working from an annotated script while dealing with a scene partner can seem a lot like juggling one ball too many. It is no easy task to act from a script while reading the words, applying your notes, and trying to listen and react to your partner all at the same time. Just knowing how to do it isn't enough; you must actually develop the skills you have been introduced to here by doing the work. So find a partner and practice these skills together. Keep in mind that mastery takes a lot of time and a lot of repetition. Patience and perseverance are also skills, essential to the development of any craft—including the craft of acting.

◇◇◇

PART TWO

Analysis Plus Synthesis

◇◇

CHAPTER SEVEN

The Problems Inherent in the Scene and Those You Bring to It

Let's assume that you have completed your initial analysis of a script in the way we've explored in this book, and must now put into practice what your analysis has suggested you do. Especially at first, it will be difficult to tell how well you are succeeding. What others see and hear you doing may be quite different than what you think you are doing. It will take time and much feedback before you can sense independently how those watching you perceive you and the work you do. And you have to be willing to hear the feedback and use it to understand how what you do comes off to those watching.

As you are learning to put your work on its feet, any of the following problems may keep you from successfully executing your well-thought-out choices:

- A problem making the story clear
- A problem making the story exciting
- A problem behaving believably
- A problem listening and reacting in the moment

- A problem using physicality
- A problem using space and props effectively
- A problem playing a stated objective or tactic
- A problem making positive choices
- A problem executing actions believably
- A problem responding to what is going on in the story (apart from the dialogue being spoken)
- A problem finding and delivering operative words that advance the story and help attain the stated objective
- A problem setting up and/or delivering a punch line
- A problem personalizing and coloring words and phrases effectively
- A problem distinguishing between what is important and what is not
- A problem recognizing what needs to be played or emphasized and what does not
- A problem recognizing and employing effectively the qualities you bring to a role naturally

How might these problems arise? Let's look at them a little more closely.

A problem making the story clear

Most of the time this results from a failure to apply your analysis in an effective way. Your focus may have strayed from your conflict and objectives, or you may be missing or failing to play the significant moments often found in beat endings and transitional moments.

A problem making the story exciting

It is always an actor's job to make the story you are telling as compelling as possible. That means you must find the conflict even where it seems not to exist (in exposition, for instance), and maximize the urgency and stakes where they are present. In other words, actors often fail to find the urgency in what seems to be ordinary, and fail to deliver the urgency and stakes of a situation when they are clearly there.

A problem behaving believably

Failing to be believable is *the* capital crime in acting, and is to be avoided at all costs. It may happen as a result of not playing your objective, failing to listen and react in the moment, focusing on your lines rather than on your partner, a discomfort with your body from general self-consciousness or because you don't know what your body should be doing, or playing actions that do not match what seems to be going on in the story.

A problem listening and reacting in the moment

Ultimately, it is your ability to listen and react moment by moment that makes you seem believable on stage. Unfortunately, as an actor you have many potentially distracting balls to juggle—the story, the words, the objectives, and the blocking, just to name a few—so it's not surprising that beginning actors commonly struggle here. If you're not a good listener in your real life, or don't listen on stage naturally because of all the other things you must think about, then learning to listen, or to quickly free your concentration for listening by efficiently taking care of your other responsibilities, is essential.

A problem using physicality

You must be able to tell the story of the play with your body as well as with your words. That means gesturing, touching people and things, and moving toward or away from them, as well as reacting physically to such cues from others. Your own physical awkwardness can keep you from being believable on stage, particularly when playing a character who does not share the kinds of physical inhibitions you may possess.

A problem using space and props effectively

In real life, people seldom stand in the middle of a room and talk. In the studio, actors as characters often do. When you don't use your space on stage effectively, you lose the opportunity to shape your story through what you do and how you do it. You move from one place to another for a reason; you do business for a reason; you do it in a particular way for a reason; you make and avoid eye contact for a reason; you touch and gesture for a reason. Remember, what you do, when you do it, and how you do it tells an audience and the actor/character you're on stage with what you are thinking and feeling from moment to moment and helps advance the story. Human beings use their whole bodies to communicate. If you fail to use space, what's in the space, and what you know about human behavior within a space, you are acting from the neck up.

A problem playing a stated objective or tactic

You must play your objectives and/or tactics at all times. That can and will happen only when you select ones that you can actually play. Playing the right objective or tactic keeps you on the railroad track of the story and makes your work clear and compelling. It also helps you make choices that an audience will believe.

A problem making positive choices

A good objective or tactic—that is, an objective or tactic that will work effectively—is one that actually gets you closer to achieving your overall objective. To insult someone, for instance, is not a good objective or tactic if your stated goal is to make someone like you. If, however, your overall objective is to make someone feel terrible, then insulting is a positive objective. You must always play tactics and objectives that get you toward what you need.

A problem executing actions believably

As a rule of thumb, actors should do only one thing at a time. In life we can sometimes multitask, but trying to do two things at once on stage usually means we will be neither clear nor believable. This is true in regard to playing a psychological action or a physical one. Actors sometimes forget that physical actions have beginnings, middles, and ends, and in the midst of trying to play two actions at once, or switching from one to another, they sometimes skip a step in the process that in life we never fail to do.

A problem responding to what is going on in the story (apart from the dialogue being spoken)

The story is seldom contained in the dialogue alone. Sometimes beginning actors are so focused on the dialogue they must say that they fail to pick up on other cues in the story being told. If, for instance, you entered a room where things were in serious disarray, you would notice this. Beginning actors, focused on their dialogue, might fail to do so.

A problem finding and delivering operative words that advance the story and help attain the stated objective

In life we naturally emphasize the words that are most important in getting us what we want or in communicating our feelings and ideas. Verbs are of particular use in communicating what we need. When actors fail to deliver their operative words effectively, their objectives will not come through clearly, nor will they sound believable.

A problem setting up and/or delivering a punch line

Closely related to the problem just mentioned, in comedies especially, certain words must be emphasized to set up a punch line, and specific words in the punch line make the line funny or witty. If an actor fails to recognize these operative words or fails to emphasize them, the joke will not be funny. You don't have to be funny, by the way, to get a laugh. But you can't step on what's funny by ignoring the mechanics.

A problem personalizing and coloring words and phrases effectively

Even when we are not directly expressing a need or telling a joke, we color and emphasize particular words in daily speech, painting word pictures and communicating thoughts and feelings. When actors fail to do so, they come off as vague and unbelievable, especially when playing important moments. Actors sometimes spontaneously hit those words, but it is the actor's responsibility to use the words the playwright has given us effectively, and therefore deliberately.

A problem distinguishing between what is important and what is not

It is your job to always tell the best story you can. But some things are more important than others in making the story clear and compelling. You must be able to recognize the difference. If you make everything important, then nothing will seem to be so. If you make nothing important, then you will seem boring or uninvested. Good storytellers must know what needs to be emphasized and what does not.

A problem recognizing what needs to be played or emphasized and what does not

Unlike in life, where you have no obligation to make clear what you are thinking and feeling at any given time, as actors you are charged with telling the story. Therefore, you must reveal your thoughts and feelings to the degree necessary to advance the overall story and the story of your character. You cannot tell everything at every moment, however. Therefore, it is your obligation to figure out what things you can and should be communicating at every moment. What does the audience already know that needs no further explanation by you? What does the audience know about you through other characters or by what has been built in by the playwright? What have you already communicated? What needs to be communicated here and now? How do you accomplish that? Finding these answers requires craft, experience, and a lot of practice.

A problem recognizing and employing effectively the qualities you bring to a role naturally

If you don't know how you come off to an audience, you don't know what things you need to emphasize in order to make the story and your character clear. Only when you understand the qualities you naturally possess or seem to communicate to an audience will you know where you can save your energy rather than trying to communicate what is already clear. On the other hand, some roles require characteristics that you may not naturally possess or express. In those cases, your choices and execution will need to convey those aspects of your character that you don't naturally bring to the role.

So, now that you have a clearer picture of the problems many young actors face, which of those listed above seem most pertinent to you? Which of them seem to keep getting in your way? If you are studying in a class, then your teacher has probably made particular observations about your work more than once. As a student working hard to develop your skills, it is your job to listen for repetition of such comments, so you can face the issues they identify head on. If you don't study acting in a class situation, then pay attention for repetition in the kinds of notes a director gives you. You are likely to find several running themes in the notes you are given—if you consciously look for them.

If you didn't recognize any of the issues mentioned above as your own, then it's time to start listening harder for them. Believe me, they are there. Every actor has them. Keep in mind that no one you work with expects you to be perfect. That is a burden that artists often put only on themselves. But it is your job to solve not only the problems of the script, but also the problems that you as an actor bring to the work. That is what rehearsal is for. It is your opportunity to work out those challenges—so it will be more helpful to pinpoint them and work with them than to pretend that they don't exist. If you do recognize some of the problems listed above in yourself, then you obviously want to be spending some of your class time and rehearsal on the things that most need your attention. Being able to recognize what your biggest problems are is the first step in solving them. Finding scenes that give you the opportunity to work on those issues is what this second part of the book is all about.

Each of the scenes in this section was written to give you an opportunity to deal, in practical form, with many of the issues that beginning actors often trip over. Examine each of them closely, even if you won't be able to put all of them up in class as fully realized scenes. Each scene contains many challenging problems that will help build your skills and stretch you. At the same time, the issues, relationships, and situations you will encounter in these scenes will likely feel accessible to you, because the characters live in a world you are familiar with. You will be able to draw on your life experience and your understanding of human nature to inform your choices.

In order to get the most out of these etudes, you'll want to work through them in a scene study class. In that environment, you will be expected not only to do your analysis homework, but also to apply that

120

analysis to the next step of your work as an actor—choice making and execution. That means you will have to go through the entire acting process by carrying out the choices you make in terms of actions—both psychological and physical. It will require you to play effective objectives and tactics, and carry out those objectives and tactics through what you do physically.

You will need to make many other important choices as well. You will need to decide what your playing area should look like so that you can tell the story in the best possible way—clearly, believably, and compellingly. The set that you create will need to serve your storytelling obligations and help justify the things you say and how you say them. You will need to create physical places to go to and move from. You will also need to decide what props to use and how to use them effectively. You will need to decide what your character should wear, and how your character will move and speak. You will have to work on all these things and rehearse them so well that ultimately you can forget about them. At that point you will be listening and reacting in the moment because the things that you previously worked on will be embedded in your muscle memory. At that point, you will be living in the moment where the real magic in acting can happen.

The scenes that follow were written in the form of a daisy-chain play. This kind of dramatic work is built on a series of two-character scenes in which character A and B have the first scene together, then character B stays on with character C in the next scene, then character C with D, and so on until the last character introduced meets with character A in the final scene. Ultimately, each of the characters appears in two scenes. My writing partner, Alan Haehnel, and I set out to create a set of etudes covering a wide range of acting situations. Ultimately, it was our intention to expose students to as broad a range of basic acting problems as possible. These etudes are chock-full of the kinds of tasks that beginning actors are likely to find most challenging.

You will find many examples of the kinds of problems we've just been looking at embedded into the fabric of each scene you encounter.

You can work through any of these etudes on its own, or you can incorporate the context created by the play as a whole. It will be up to you and/or your teacher (if you are using this material in a class situation) to decide whether to work on each scene in relation to the overall play, or to make choices based solely on the information available in the individual scene. If you choose to see each scene as an independent entity, you will have to make choices about the backstory or given circumstances that justify the action and dialogue and help tell the story clearly. If you choose to see the scene in terms of the entire play, you will have to make choices that are consistent with what you know about the overall action and backstory, as you would do with any other scene that is part of a greater whole. Either way you will be challenged by the problems offered by each scene.

You will also find that there is one additional scene included in this set of etudes—one that violates the daisy-chain premise. In this scene, all of the characters come together for the first and only time. The scene was added after the rest of the play had been completed. It was written, not as an etude, but at the request of the director of the first workshop production of the play, to give the work a more complete arc and a better feeling of closure. This final scene cannot stand alone as the other scenes in this collection can. There are simply too many references and relationship details for an audience to grasp without having seen the daisy-chain scenes. I have included the scene, however, not only so that you can see how the play might work as a unified entity, but also because it may help you make choices elsewhere in the play. Reading it will tell you more about who the characters are and how they have changed by the end of the story arc. If you are working on a particular scene in the context of the greater whole, you may want to include what you learned from the last scene. Keep in mind that multi-character scenes are not ideal for a scene study class, of course, and I do not recommend you take it on, unless you are being directed. (If, by the way, your teacher or director does take on the play for production, you will need to procure the rights through Playscripts.)

If you happen to get your hands on the acting edition of *Toward the Sun*, you will find a note about the order of scenes in our workshop production. We discovered that the play, having been written as a set of learning tools and not with the overall arc of a comprehensive story, did not build toward an ultimate climax in a completely satisfying way. Instead, some of the individual scenes proved to be more climactic than the overall arc of the play. In trying to solve this problem, our director not only asked for the additional scene, but he also experimented with the arrangement of the scenes. We had more ideas than we had time to explore, but ultimately our production settled on a non-chronological arrangement of scenes that we felt made for a better overall arc. The point here is, if you choose to work on this play in its entirety as a class project, you should feel free to experiment with its order of scenes and structure. In fact, we encourage you, as part of your analysis and synthesis training, to examine the play in terms of its overall arc and try to figure out how it might work best for your audience. You will learn a lot (as we did) from whatever experimentation you choose to explore.

Before you do so, however, let's consider these scenes as individual etudes for your development.

Earlier in this chapter, I asked you to try to identify the kinds of problems you think are most prevalent in your work as it currently stands. Whatever those problems are, there are particular kinds of scenes that are most likely to give you the best opportunities to work on those issues. For each common problem we examined, you'll find a type of scene described below that will help you address it.

- **A problem making the story clear**—a simple, clear-cut, cause-and-effect scene that presents discoveries or new information

- **A problem making the story exciting**—a life-and-death situation demanding urgency and high stakes

- **A problem behaving believably**—a scene with a strong conflict where clear, strong objectives must be played, or a non-climactic scene in which there is a good deal of business and physical activity

- **A problem listening and reacting in the moment**—a scene that requires constant reacting to what the other character says and does

- **A problem using physicality**—a scene set in a realistic and specific space where dialogue comes out of believable ongoing business or physical activity, a scene requiring physical contact and movement from place to place, or a scene requiring specific use of props

- **A problem using space and props effectively**—same as above

- **A problem playing a stated objective or tactic**—a scene that has a simple, clear conflict

- **A problem making positive choices**—a scene built around an argument or discussion of an issue

- **A problem executing actions believably**—a scene with a simple, clear-cut objective to play and a step-by-step progression, or a scene where what is done physically is as important as or more important than the dialogue itself

- **A problem responding to what is going on in the story (apart from the dialogue being spoken)**—a scene where the other character has considerable physical action and business that informs and colors his or her dialogue and/or requires your attention, or a scene where the actor does more listening yet has a big arc to travel

- **A problem finding and delivering operative words that advance the story and help attain the stated objective**—a scene with a very strong objective, or a scene where most of your dialogue is in reaction to what is said to you
- **A problem setting up and/or delivering a punch line**—a witty or funny scene in which your character's words are used specifically to make winning points
- **A problem personalizing and coloring words and phrases effectively**—a scene in which the dialogue consists of personal information and/or lists
- **A problem distinguishing between what is important and what is not**—a conversational scene where seemingly there is little at stake
- **A problem recognizing what needs to be played or emphasized and what does not**—a scene where your character has either a lot of dialogue or very little dialogue
- **A problem recognizing and employing effectively the qualities you bring to a role naturally**—a scene where you identify closely with the character you are playing, or you play a character as far removed from you as possible

You will notice that each of the following scenes is accompanied by a list of characteristics and challenges present in that scene. The list is intended to help you select scenes that may address your particular acting problem or problems. That does not mean you should ignore the scene if one of your acknowledged problems doesn't seem to be present; each list will, however, give you clues as to the kinds of obligations you will have as an actor if you choose that particular scene to work on.

You will also find that each scene is followed by a set of notes that addresses some of the challenges and issues you will find in that particular scene. It is intended as an aid or reinforcement to the analysis skills you are developing as well as an instructive view of the scene from the perspective of the writer/director/acting teacher who composed them. Feel free to ignore the notes altogether, or look at them after you have done your own independent work. Remember, your goal is to develop your own reliable craft—one that allows you to work independently, economically, and with confidence. So use the commentary in any way that best serves those goals.

Toward the Sun

By Alan Haehnel and
Bruce Miller

◇◇◇

CHAPTER EIGHT

Scene 1:
Fame and Fortune

Issues You Will Need to Consider:

High stakes
Life-and-death urgency
Strong conflict and objectives
Obstacles
Big arc to scene
Business and physical activity
Storytelling through physicality
Physical actions requiring attention of other character
Business and physical activity informs dialogue
Constant tactical changes
Listening with all senses required
Dialogue in response to what is said to you
Use of wit, operatives, and punch lines
Personal information
Discoveries, new information, wins and losses
Large amount of dialogue
Monologues

◇◇◇◇◇◇◇◇◇◇◇◇◇◇◇

Open to COURTNEY *and* ALLISON *lying on two rock platforms,* COURTNEY *on the higher one.* ALLISON *wears a bathing suit with a T-shirt covering the top.* COURTNEY *is lying on her stomach, her bikini top untied.*

COURTNEY I don't like this. (*Pause*) This is like lying on a rock.

ALLISON You *are* lying on a rock.

COURTNEY I don't like it. How's the rock down there?

ALLISON Soft. Very soft.

COURTNEY Right, like lying on a cloud, huh?

(*A chime sounds on* ALLISON'*s phone, indicating she has a text.* ALLISON *reads it.*)

ALLISON Yeah. Bud says you're a…let me quote here…"a fuckin' coward."

COURTNEY Fuck Bud. I don't see him up here. What time is it?

ALLISON 2:57.

COURTNEY I said three o'clock. I said I'd do it at three o'clock, not 2:57.

ALLISON It just turned 58.

COURTNEY Same diff.

(*Another chime on* ALLISON'*s phone.*)

ALLISON   From Anna: "Are you doing this or what?"

(COURTNEY *sits up, holding her bikini top to her chest, and shouts over the edge.*)

COURTNEY   Eat me. Eat me! I don't see any of you up here! It's not even time yet!

ALLISON   I don't think they can hear you.

COURTNEY   Relax, assholes! I'll go when I'm ready!

ALLISON   Wow. Nice language. From the f-ing valedictorian, no less. What would your mother say?

COURTNEY   She'd say she was proud of me for asserting myself. Especially under such stressful circumstances.

ALLISON   Not the Mrs. Matheson I know.

COURTNEY   She may ride my ass in public, but when we're alone, my shit don't stink.

ALLISON   Yeah, right.

COURTNEY   That's right. With her I can do no wrong.

ALLISON   And I'm sure you shared with her the fact that you were coming up here.

COURTNEY   Of course. I tell her every little thing.

ALLISON   Jesus.

COURTNEY   I say, "Mother, I tried weed last night and I found it very enjoyable."

ALLISON   Yeah, right.

COURTNEY   I say, "Mother, Troy and I will be downstairs making out and I'm not sure if he brought a condom." And just this morning, before I left, I said, "Mother, I'm going to make that quarry jump today." And she said, "Hope you're planning to break a record if you're going to do such risky things with your precious spare time."

ALLISON   Right.

COURTNEY   No, really, she did say, "Okay, baby, I'm so glad you're leading such an adventurous life. I'm behind you every step of the way, and I totally trust your judgment. I look forward to basking in your glory."

ALLISON   Bull. Shit.

COURTNEY   "And by the way so does your father. He loves you every bit as much as I do, baby."

ALLISON   Yeah, right. Are you high or something?

COURTNEY   I am very high. High atop Mount Granite quarry.

(*Another chime from* ALLISON*'s phone.*)

ALLISON   It's from Bud again. He says you are sooo, and I quote, "Bluck bluck, chicken!"

COURTNEY   And he is sooo blucking without imagination. (*Yelling over the edge.*) Hey, Buddy, can't you come up with anything more interesting? There are other insults in the English language that reference cowardice, you morons!

ALLISON   Courtney, there's no way they're hearing you.

COURTNEY   I know there's no way they're hearing me but I desire to ululate at the peasants below nonetheless. Hey, I'm screaming at you, you pussies!

ALLISON   That was imaginative. What's ululate?

COURTNEY   Scream or something. Whew. That's a long ways down. That's a big-ass boulder between me and immortality. Be sure to quote that on Facebook.

ALLISON   Yeah, that one down there. That's where the mortals jump from. No jumping there for you, though. Olympus proper for you. Get past that boulder down there and it's a cakewalk.

COURTNEY   How 'bout we do this together?

ALLISON   No way.

COURTNEY   You can jump from down there.

ALLISON   Not a prayer. I think twice about steppin' off high curbs.

COURTNEY   So why am I doing this again?

ALLISON   Because you are Super Courtney! Who does it all! Parties on Friday night and aces her SAT's the next morning. Gives a kick-ass graduation speech that has everybody in tears and then eggs Dr. P's house that same night. Who does that kind of stuff. Wait a minute—Courtney!

COURTNEY   Get out. I'm not that bad.

ALLISON   No, you're that good. I'm serious, you do it all, including the self-promotion. Like Facebook. Join me at the quarry when I break the quarry record. And the masses turn out to see you.

COURTNEY   And you hate me, right?

ALLISON   What are you talking about?

COURTNEY   I don't know. Sometimes I think everybody resents me.

ALLISON   That's just crazy talk.

COURTNEY   What if I didn't do all this crap? What if I decided I just wanted to stay home and watch infomercials and stuff my face until I weighed three hundred pounds?

ALLISON   Then you wouldn't be Courtney.

COURTNEY   Sometimes I just want to tell everybody to go fuck themselves! Go find someone else to live through. Sometimes I feel like a goddamned circus act, you know? Courtney's three-ring circus. Got one routine for my parents, another one for the colleges, another one for my friends. But what if I just stopped doing this shit? Just turned into ordinary Courtney? I don't think anybody'd be interested in that, do you? (ALLISON*'s phone chimes again.*) I know, I know, it's time. Don't even bother to look at it. What time is it?

ALLISON   3:03.

COURTNEY   Uh-oh. White Rabbit.

ALLISON   Courtney, listen...

COURTNEY   No, no, no, don't worry about it. Time to do this. Get myself psyched. It's Courtney time! Turn that camera on, Watson, it's time to make history. Another exciting adventure to chronicle.

ALLISON You sure?

COURTNEY Sure I'm sure! I'm fine. (*An improvised song*) It's late. It's late, for a very important date. My momma says I'm fine, my daddy says I'm fine, I had a little drink of some mighty fine wine. Hey, are you recording?

ALLISON Not yet.

COURTNEY Turn on the cell. Get that damn camera rolling. (*Shaking, loosening up*) Where's my water bottle? Couple swigs here. (*She chugs from her water bottle.*) Ah! Right! Now we're cooking! Maudlin moment's behind me, and now it's time to *prove it* again! Record breakin' prove it, mode! I will do anything. Just say I can't.

ALLISON You can't.

COURTNEY Dare me, bet me! I WILL DO IT! You getting this?

ALLISON I'm rolling.

COURTNEY Bet me I won't flash my tits!

ALLISON Betcha you won't flash your tits!

COURTNEY I will take that bet. (COURTNEY *pulls her bikini top down, exposing her breasts.*) And I do! Woo-woo!

ALLISON Courtney, come on!

COURTNEY Gotta prove it, right?

ALLISON Keep your clothes on.

COURTNEY Are we good to go? Yeah? Okay then, here we go!

ALLISON Wait, wait, wait! Are you really going now?

COURTNEY What do you mean? It is time for another record-breaking moment!

ALLISON Wait a sec. Let me text down to them to make sure they're ready. Everybody wants to shoot this.

(COURTNEY *takes another drink from her water bottle.*)

COURTNEY Get 'em ready. Line 'em up, and get 'em ready. Courtney's coming to life. How many are down there, anyway?

ALLISON I don't know; your guess is as good as mine.

COURTNEY Not without my contacts in, it's not. It's just one big blur down there. HEY YOU, BLUR PEOPLE! Get ready for touchdown! Who are you texting?

ALLISON Troy.

COURTNEY He's not down there.

ALLISON Are you sure?

COURTNEY He's at work.

ALLISON No, he's not. He gets done at two o'clock, right?

COURTNEY How do you know?

ALLISON I…thought he told me that one time. I mean, I've seen him pulling out of the store sometimes before three.

COURTNEY Huh. (ALLISON*'s phone chimes.*) Is that him?

ALLISON Uh, yeah.

COURTNEY What's he say?

ALLISON That…he's not down there. I'll text Anna.

COURTNEY You do that. You text that girl Anna. She's down there. Do you know when she gets off work?

ALLISON Whaddaya mean?

COURTNEY Right. Didn't think so.

ALLISON What are you talkin' about?

COURTNEY Nothing. It means you don't know when Anna gets off work. I don't either. I don't even know *if* Anna works. Maybe she sits at home stuffin' her face and watchin' infomercials. Maybe she's living the dream!

(ALLISON*'s phone chimes.*)

ALLISON Everybody's ready.

COURTNEY Everybody's ready. That's great. That's great. Everybody's ready. I'm ready! You ready?

ALLISON (*Filming*) Ready.

(COURTNEY *takes in a deep breath, closes her eyes, stumbles a bit.*)

ALLISON You okay?

COURTNEY Yeah, yeah, yeah, perfect. On three, here we go. One, two...ah! Jesus Christ!

(COURTNEY *backs away from the edge and crouches suddenly.*)

ALLISON What? What's going on?

COURTNEY Didn't you feel that gust? It hit me like a fucking— Jesus, it was like a...gust!

ALLISON I didn't feel it.

COURTNEY Didn't...? It was like a blast of *"don't do this thing"*?

ALLISON No. I mean, it's completely possible that I just didn't feel it down...

(COURTNEY *takes another swig from her bottle.*)

COURTNEY I'm not jumping. Forget it.

ALLISON Hey, it was just...

COURTNEY I'm not jumping! With it gusting like that, it could blow me right into the rocks. Forget it.

ALLISON You could time it.

COURTNEY Time it?

ALLISON Yeah. If...if you see the wind in the trees over there or rippling on the water...

COURTNEY I told you. I don't have my contacts in! I'm practically blind. I told you, Jesus. Why are you so all about me doing this?

ALLISON I'm not.

COURTNEY Good. Cause I ain't! (ALLISON*'s phone goes off again.*) Just text them it's off, okay? Tell them that Courtney the performing seal isn't doing her show today, all right?

ALLISON Courtney, listen...

COURTNEY Now you'll have time to grab a quickie with Troy since he's already out of work.

ALLISON What are you talking about?

COURTNEY   You can have him, by the way.

ALLISON   Courtney, stop. Come on.

COURTNEY   I am not jumping.

ALLISON   Okay. That's cool. You don't have to.

COURTNEY   Thanks. Bitch!

(*The phone goes off again.*)

COURTNEY   Tell 'em to fuck off! I'm not doing it! Text them to fuck off, Bitch!

ALLISON   Look, look, I'm shutting it off. It doesn't matter. Just sit down for a minute. What's going on?

COURTNEY   Nothin'. That wind. It scared the shit out of me. It was like...all of a sudden death was looking me right in the face. You know? No. How would you know? Cold chill went right through me.

ALLISON   Hell, Court, I get that feeling sitting on a Ferris wheel, never mind trying to get me on a roller coaster or anything like that. I can't even come close to doing the shit you do.

COURTNEY   Good. You get it. Just like the Ferris wheel. Fuck you; fuck this. Man, I'm feeling pukey.

ALLISON   Just give it a second. Relax. It'll pass. And then you can jump. I mean, if you want.

COURTNEY   What the fuck? I just told you! I am not...

ALLISON   Courtney, you have never backed down from anything in your life, not since I've known you. You do shit, you're right, but it's not all about pleasing other people. You do shit, shit that other people wouldn't do, because you are Courtney. Because you grab life by the balls. (*She gestures as if grabbing a pair of balls.*) These are balls, by the way. It's who you are. It's your dope, girl.

COURTNEY Wait a second. Why are you so all about this? What the fuck is your angle?

ALLISON I don't have an angle. I just don't want you to climb down from here because of a stupid gust of wind. You know? I don't want you to get down from here and regret it. Lose the coverage. Lose points toward immortality, you know. Because you know you will. I'm just being your friend here.

COURTNEY Okay, *friend*. I do this, and you jump off the lower rock down there. I mean it.

ALLISON Not a chance. I told you that already. I am totally comfortable with being a coward. You, on the other hand, are not and never will be.

COURTNEY Do it for Troy.

ALLISON What?

COURTNEY I gotta pee.

ALLISON Do it on the way down.

COURTNEY Where's my water bottle? One more for the road.

ALLISON Here it is. (*Withholding the bottle.*) Are you going to do this?

COURTNEY Yeah, I'm going to do it.

140

ALLISON   Why?

COURTNEY   Because I'm Courtney and I do shit.

ALLISON   That's right. And because I don't have a life without you.

COURTNEY   Pitiful.

ALLISON   I could use a sip.

COURTNEY   Uh—that's water with a kick.

(ALLISON *takes a swig from* COURTNEY*'s bottle and gasps.*)

ALLISON   What is that?

COURTNEY   Water. With a little vodka.

ALLISON   I don't think so—try vodka with a little water.

(COURTNEY *takes another drink.*)

COURTNEY   Yeah, maybe that was the formula. I'm going back up.

ALLISON   Wait a second—hold on. How much have you had to drink, anyway?

COURTNEY   Just turn your phone back on and get your camera ready!

ALLISON   Courtney, how much have you had to drink?

COURTNEY   Alert the masses. I'm doing this. (*She slips.*) Whoa.

ALLISON   Hey, maybe this is a bad idea after all.

COURTNEY   No, no, no, I'm fine. You're right. A little breeze in the face, fuck it. I can handle it.

ALLISON   I don't know.

COURTNEY   Make up your mind, Allie! You were the one giving me the inspirational speech. What the fuck!

ALLISON   Yeah, well, that's before I knew you were drinking. Maybe you shouldn't be wasted when you do this.

COURTNEY   I am cone stold sober...sorta. Get out your phone. Turn it on.

ALLISON   Are you sure?

COURTNEY   Yeah I'm sure. Bring it on! It's time for the Courtney show. (ALLISON*'s phone chimes again.*) What are they texting?

ALLISON   Just more of the same shit—hurry up, what's taking so long, Bud calling you chickenshit.

COURTNEY   Text 'em. Get those cell phones clicking. This will be epic!

ALLISON   I should never have pushed you to do this. I'm not liking this any more.

COURTNEY   Are you rolling?

ALLISON   Yeah, but I'm still not liking it.

COURTNEY   Well, I have to pee really bad now, so I'm going. (*The phone chimes.*) All systems go down there?

ALLISON   All systems go. Are you sure?

COURTNEY   122 percent. So I'm your idol, right?

ALLISON   Totally.

COURTNEY   You're full of shit! Whew, there's that wind again.

ALLISON   Don't do it, then!

COURTNEY   Fuck you! Like you said—just a breeze. I can handle it. On three, now—count it with me, darlin'! One, two, three!

ALLISON (*With* COURTNEY)   One, two, three!

(COURTNEY *jumps with a yell.*)

Notes on the Scene

This scene, like two others in *Toward the Sun*, is set on a cliff, high above a quarry. This was not an accident. Placing the scene in a dangerously high locale ensures that there are also extremely high stakes, because of the inherent threat of falling. The choice of setting was inspired by *Precipice*, a ten-minute play written by William Mastrosimone. I have been using that play in my introductory scene study class for years now because, to put it simply, the play is a perfect teaching tool for beginning actors. The action takes place high in the mountains above a precipice just before nightfall. The stakes are life and death because the characters must decide whether to jump across a fogged-out divide. If the characters jump, they could fall to their deaths. If they stay, they will freeze to death. As a result of these given circumstances, beginning actors won't have to find ways of making the stakes high; they are built in. And because the characters

143

are in a life-threatening situation, the objectives are simple, clear, and direct. Yet, every time I use the scene in class, the actors, no matter how savvy, seem to forget or can't maintain those life-and-death stakes—so the scene is neither compelling nor believable. And certainly the script fails to be served—a total violation of the definition of good acting. It is a great first lesson for actors.

For these reasons, Alan and I wanted to create several etudes that would provide actors with similar traps. The quarry setting does so. Both characters in this scene must deal with a physical environment that remains dangerous at all times, and the actors playing Courtney and Allison, though their attitudes about the location differ, must never forget that fact. Each of their lives is at risk, and the way each of them deals with the environment tells the audience a great deal about them. The way the actors as characters handle their environment is revealed through their choice of physical actions. But, unlike in *Precipice*, what these characters say is often at odds with what their physical actions tell us, particularly in the case of Courtney.

The objectives and tactics of the characters in "Fame and Fortune" are far less obvious than those in *Precipice*. Each character has obstacles and secrets that keep her from pursuing her objectives in a direct manner. Therefore, listening and deciding how to react at every moment in order to find the next tactic is critically important throughout. For the actors playing Courtney and Allison, listening for new information and making discoveries as to what to say and do next become incredibly important to reaching their goals. The characters play a game of chess where the give-and-take and tactical maneuvering create a very large arc. The scene challenges the actors to connect the dots from moment to moment so that they can build that arc with clarity. At the top of the scene Courtney is bold and confident. By the end, she is masking her fear, and not so successfully at that. Allison starts the scene as a cheerleader for jumping, and ends up doing everything she can to keep the jump from happening. It is up to the actors to make those journeys as compelling and believable as possible.

Scene 1 has a title. Did you note it? Titles of plays can be important and extremely helpful to actors trying to make their way through a script analysis. Titles often reflect something important about the meaning of a play and/or give insights into the author's take on the characters. I spent a great deal of time on the title of each of the etudes you will find here in order to reinforce that idea. Beginning actors often skip over the name of the play—and of the playwright, too. Suck the marrow out of any title. It may prove nourishing. And be sure to research the author. Often you will find themes and characteristics in a playwright's body of work that can help inform your choices in a particular play. Be on the lookout, too, for ideas that run through an entire play, so that you can make choices that bring those ideas out. What connections can you draw between the title "Fame and Fortune" and the characters and ideas you've encountered in this play?

Obviously, the location of this scene is vitally important. That has already been established. But how the actors create that setting physically and move through it is equally key. Dealing with the environment is a major storytelling obligation and is not always reflected in the dialogue. So is dealing with your scene partner physically. Courtney drinks. How will the actor reflect that through her body work? You must build tension through the physical storytelling process as much as through the dialogue.

Allison is far more uncomfortable moving through the physical space than Courtney. How will she reflect that? Courtney speaks to the crowd below. How is that different from speaking to Allison? Allison switches back and forth from Courtney to her cell phone. What are the differences between the two? Etc.

Subtext is very important in this scene as well. Obstacles and secrets must be dealt with. Why does Courtney choose now to rail against

145

the expectations of her audience? Why is she drinking? How can she let the audience know what she is all about without telegraphing it to Allison? How do we do such things in life? Allison has a secret agenda for wanting Court to jump. How can she keep that a secret from Courtney and yet get the audience to believe her when, in the arc of the story, she reveals her real reasons for pushing Courtney so hard? These are significant acting challenges.

So is making the arc of the story clear and believable. How does Courtney believably handle the arc of her drinking? How does Allison make the journey from pushing Court to trying to stop her from jumping? Where are the storytelling moments along the way? The give-and-take in the dialogue, the use of wit, the landing of punch lines, and the reactions to moments of victory, defeat, and discovery are all vital to making the arc of the story believable and compelling. These are two extremely intelligent and verbal young women. The challenge is to bring them to life and make their words and actions reveal the story.

<<<<<<<<<<<<<<<<<<<<<<<<<<<<<<<<<<<<<<<<<<<<<<<<<<<<<>

Scene 2:
Siege of Troy

Issues You Will Need to Consider:

Simple, clear, cause-and-effect scene
Strong objectives but not literal life and death
Clear tactics
Obstacles
Wins, losses, discoveries
Listening and reacting
Reacting to new info/discoveries
Business, but limited physical action
Physical acting to show thoughts and feelings
Use of wit, punch lines, verbal battle

<<<<<<<<<<<<<<<<>

The waiting room at a hospital. ALLISON *sits on a couch with her eyes closed.* TROY *enters, carrying a backpack. He sits down near* ALLISON, *trying not to disturb her. After a few seconds,* ALLISON *opens her eyes.*

TROY   Hey.

(ALLISON *hugs* TROY *desperately.*)

ALLISON Oh, God, Troy. It was awful. So awful.

TROY Shhh. It's okay.

ALLISON God. God.

(*They break from the hug.*)

TROY How's she doing?

ALLISON She hasn't woken up yet. Her parents are with her. You should check with the nurse and see if you can go in.

TROY I'll...I don't want to crowd her parents. I'll wait. How're *you* doing?

ALLISON How do you think? I must look like hell.

TROY No, you look...you look good.

ALLISON Liar.

TROY I'm not...really. You always.... I mean, you're tired, obviously. I can see that.

ALLISON Yeah.

TROY Have you had anything to eat? Or drink?

ALLISON No...yeah,...I think so. I don't remember.

TROY I'll take that as a no. (TROY *unzips his backpack and lays out the food he has brought.*) We've got a cinnamon-raisin bagel from Dunkin' Donuts, cream cheese on the side so you can apply it one bite at a time; one Vitamin Water, flavor Revive with potassium and vitamin B...

148

ALLISON How did you... this is like my favorite stuff.

TROY Yeah, I know. I been watchin' you. You know, in case you hadn't noticed. (*As* TROY *continues to lay out the picnic for* ALLISON, *she watches and begins to cry.*) We'll just pour a little of this in a cup for you. This was a very good year for Vitamin Water. (*Looking at the label.*) Or a very good month, anyway. What else? Ah, yes, for your further dining pleasure, we have a single Lindt chocolate, extra dark. Feel free to indulge, but I insist you eat at least half your bagel first. (*Noticing* ALLISON *crying.*) Hey, what is it?

ALLISON She could die, Troy. You shouldn't be doing this. You shouldn't be doing anything for me. What if she dies?

TROY Look, she's stable, right?

ALLISON With an injury like that, stable could become unstable any second. The doctor said it's too early to tell anything for sure. She's in a coma, Troy. Courtney is in a fucking coma. (*They sit silently for a few seconds.* TROY *leans forward and begins to cut the bagel into small chunks.*) What are you doing?

TROY I'm making Allison bagel bites. I've seen you do this enough; I know the technique. We cut off approximately a one-inch section of bagel, we spread on approximately a little layer of cream cheese...

ALLISON Troy.

TROY Voilà. Try one.

ALLISON I can't.

TROY You can. And you should. Come on. I sanitized my hands.

ALLISON Troy.

TROY You know you want to.

ALLISON Where have you been?

TROY What?

ALLISON What took you so long to get here, Troy?

TROY I...

ALLISON That is your girlfriend in there!

TROY I know! I just... I was working.

ALLISON It happened after you got out of work.

TROY I didn't find out until... I mean, nobody...

ALLISON Are you telling me people haven't been texting you, haven't been calling you for, like, the last five hours? I don't believe that for one second.

TROY I... I stopped to get you this...

ALLISON I'm sorry. Four hours? Where the fuck have you been?

(ALLISON *sweeps the food and* TROY'*s backpack off the table.*)

TROY Hey!

ALLISON With your girlfriend dying in the hospital you stopped to put together a fucking picnic... for me?

TROY Allison.

ALLISON Who does that? What are you thinking, asshole?

TROY I was...

150

ALLISON   Who *does* that, Troy?

TROY   I do that! I did that, okay? When I found out what happened, I...I thought about you.

ALLISON   What?

TROY   I said I thought about you. I knew Courtney was being taken care of. There was nothing I could do to help *her*. But I wondered who was taking care of you. If that makes me a total asshole, then so be it, I'm a total asshole. But I thought about *you*.

ALLISON   Jesus.

TROY   I mean, I could apologize, I guess, but my mind goes where it goes. And lately it's been going...

ALLISON   Stop.

TROY   It's been going...

ALLISON   I said stop it, Troy. Please.

(*A long silence.* TROY *begins picking up the food* ALLISON *threw on the floor.*)

ALLISON   You don't have to do that.

TROY   I'm not going to leave it for the janitor or something.

ALLISON   I made the mess. I'll clean it up later.

TROY   I'll get it.

ALLISON   You have to stop doing things for me. I'm begging you. It's wrong. It's so wrong. It makes me hurt even more than I already do.

TROY (*Rising*)   Okay. I'll just leave the rest of this food here, just in case you.... You really should eat something. And that's not me trying to do anything for you, it's just...take care of yourself. Okay?

ALLISON   Are you leaving?

TROY   Yeah. Yeah, I am.

ALLISON   You haven't even seen Courtney.

TROY   Look, I'm not exactly her father's favorite person in the world. I'll come back later when the coast is clear.

ALLISON   How are you going to know when that is?

TROY   I don't know. I'm not sure.

ALLISON   Did you really think her parents wouldn't be here?

TROY   Like I told you, I wasn't thinking about them that much, actually. I guess I wasn't thinking clearly at all. I just...

ALLISON   What?

TROY   Knew that you'd be here. But I see I read that, um, situation all wrong, too. I'm just gonna go.

ALLISON   Troy.

TROY   Yeah.

ALLISON   Come here. Sit with me.

TROY   Yeah?

ALLISON   I've been in talking to Courtney for hours, but...I need to know someone can hear me.

TROY Okay. (TROY *sits back down*.) What have you been saying to her?

ALLISON Mainly, that I'm sorry.

TROY Sorry? For what?

ALLISON Lots of stuff. Bad stuff.

TROY Like what?

ALLISON Like I made her do it. It was my fault.

TROY Hey, come on. How do you figure that?

ALLISON She wasn't going to do it. I talked her back into jumping.

TROY I hate to tell you, but this is Courtney we're talking about here. The minute she posted she was going to jump, it was a done deal.

ALLISON You weren't there. You weren't up there with her.

TROY What are you saying, that you physically pushed her off the rocks?

ALLISON No.

TROY Then she did it herself.

ALLISON I could have talked her out of it.

TROY Allison, like I said: we're talking about Courtney here.

ALLISON She stood up to do it, to jump. And she felt this... this gust of wind. It freaked her out.

TROY Really?

ALLISON   Yeah.

TROY   I'm surprised that would rattle her.

ALLISON   She was drinking. She had vodka in her water bottle. I'm not sure how much she had. But I'll tell you this: she wasn't steady, and she didn't have her contacts in. That wind really freaked her out, Troy. She was totally ready to just climb down.

TROY   So what did you tell her?

ALLISON   I didn't know about the vodka. I found that out later, when it was too late, when I'd already got her to change her mind back to doing it. I never would have...

TROY   Allison, you still haven't told me anything that would make this your fault.

ALLISON   The wind...I told her I didn't feel it. I told her it wasn't a big deal!

TROY   If you didn't...

ALLISON   I did feel it! She was right. It was gusting bad up there. I lied to her because I wanted her to jump.

TROY   Everybody did. It's not on anybody's radar that Courtney could actually get hurt. I'm sure if the whole crowd had been up there, they would have been telling her the same thing: Jump! You'll be fine.

ALLISON   They all kept texting from down below.

TROY   Texting what? "Come down from there, Courtney"?

ALLISON   No. "Do it. Don't be a chicken shit."

TROY That's what I mean. So how the fuck does that make it your fault?

ALLISON I told her that she wouldn't be able to live with herself if she didn't do it. I put it back on her. I know her, Troy. I know how to push her buttons. And I did.

TROY Okay. But it was still on her...

ALLISON But that wasn't why I was pushing so hard for her to jump.

TROY Okay....

ALLISON I had...I had money on it.

TROY What?

ALLISON I had money on it. With a lot of people. I was going to lose almost five hundred dollars if she didn't do it.

TROY Whoa.

ALLISON You see now?

TROY Yeah. Yeah, I guess I do.

ALLISON It was a sure thing. I knew she would do it. And I knew I could get her to do it if necessary.

TROY No wonder you're not hungry.

ALLISON And then there's the stuff with us.

TROY Shhhhh.

ALLISON I'm so sorry, Troy.

TROY Why are you saying that to me.

ALLISON   God, Troy, I...I could have killed Courtney. She's my friend, Troy! Your girlfriend, for god sakes. I may have killed her for a few hundred bucks!

(TROY *hugs* ALLISON *as she cries.*)

TROY   Hey, come on. She's not.... She's going to come out of this. She'll be okay.

ALLISON   You don't know that.

TROY   Come on. She's tough. She'll be okay. I mean it. She'll pull through. That's the way Courtney is. Come on, drink this.

ALLISON   I don't...

TROY   Drink. If you've been crying like this for hours, you're probably dehydrated. (ALLISON *takes a sip of the Vitamin Water, then drinks more.*) Better?

ALLISON   Yeah. I guess I was thirsty.

TROY   I can salvage most of the food. I bet if you took a bite, you'd find out you're hungry, too.

ALLISON   I don't deserve...

TROY   What? You don't deserve to eat because you had money on Courtney jumping? You're such a terrible person that you're supposed to starve to death now?

ALLISON   I don't know.

TROY   Look, me and Courtney...I don't even know how we ended up going out.

ALLISON   I can tell you that. Saturday night, May eighteenth.

156

TROY What?

ALLISON A bunch of us girls were at my house. Courtney started texting you. It was kind of a game.

TROY You were there?

ALLISON She knew you wouldn't recognize her number.

TROY I didn't. I just thought it was somebody being a jerk, you know.

ALLISON "Hey, Troy, this is your lucky day?" "For a good time, call me back."

TROY And I did ignore them for a while.

ALLISON But then she started in with the pictures. Lips, cleavage…

TROY You were really there?

ALLISON A whole bunch of us were. You didn't do so bad. You ignored the first, like, seven calls.

TROY I can't believe this.

ALLISON What did she get you with? The crotch shot with the caption, right?

TROY "Can't help liking what you see, right, Troy?" Or something like that.

ALLISON Yeah, you called after that one.

TROY Shit. What an idiot.

ALLISON Naw. It was just another one of Courtney's games. She plays to win, that's all. She picked you, she threw out the bait, and you took it.

TROY You sound mad.

ALLISON A little disappointed, maybe. Look, you're a guy.

TROY Shit. I guess I shouldn't be surprised that our whole . . . relationship was nothing more than a public party game. That's what it always felt like, too. Everything's a public show with her.

ALLISON You talking in the past tense? News flash, Troy: Courtney may be in a coma, but she's still alive. And she's still your girlfriend. Not exactly the ideal time for breaking up.

TROY Yeah. (*A pause*) It was over, Allison. I mean, if we weren't hanging with a bunch of people, we didn't even know what to do with each other.

ALLISON That's not what I heard.

TROY What did *you* hear?

ALLISON That you guys . . . had a lot of sex.

TROY I guess.

ALLISON You guess? Rumor has it that you were there, Troy.

TROY Yeah, sorta, I guess.

ALLISON What is that supposed to mean?

TROY Look, it never felt right, not from the very beginning. Yeah, we did our share of messing around, you know . . .

ALLISON Spare me the details.

TROY We had sex a few times, but that's it. Over the last couple weeks, we weren't doing it at all. We never really connected, all right? We never really had anything to say to each other.

ALLISON   Isn't that supposed to be the girl's complaint—"we never talk"? Sounds to me like the perfect deal.

TROY   Not really. Courtney felt the same way, I think. Look, it just seemed like one day I woke up and realized, "Hey, I'm Courtney's boyfriend now." I had to keep reminding myself. It never felt real or natural, for either of us.

ALLISON   Okay, fine, great. Why are we even talking about this? What does this have to do with…?

TROY   Allison, my point is that if you're looking for somebody to hate you because you had a bet on Courtney jumping, if you're looking for somebody to tell you what a terrible, selfish person you are…it ain't gonna be me.

ALLISON   Why not?

TROY   Because the best part about going out with Courtney hasn't been about Courtney. It's been about hanging out with you.

ALLISON   Great. That's another thing I can feel really bad about.

TROY   I don't. That hour when you would come by the shop. And I would barely even touch you…even though I wanted to…bad.

ALLISON   Yeah, I know. Me, too.

(TROY *leans in to kiss* ALLISON. *She moves to meet him, then backs away.*)

ALLISON   We shouldn't.

TROY   When can we?

ALLISON   Probably never! She's my best friend, and she's your girlfriend, Troy, and that makes us off limits. She's down the hall in a coma, for Christ's sake. It's wrong. It makes us bad people for even thinking about it.

TROY   Right or wrong, it's about all I do think about.

ALLISON   Well, stop. You should go in and see her. Even if it's just for a minute, even if her parents are in there, even if it feels fake. You should do it. Cause it's the right thing to do.

TROY   Allie...

ALLISON   Plus, if you don't, I'll feel even more guilty.

TROY   Okay, okay. Here's the deal. I will go in and see Courtney for as long as I can stand her parents staring me down. But you have to eat something while I'm gone. And then I'm going to come back and stay here with you.

ALLISON   No. You're going to say good-bye to me on your way out the door.

TROY   Oh, really?

ALLISON   I'm not going to deny the feelings are there, Troy, but the timing's wrong.

TROY   I can be patient.

ALLISON   Go. See her.

TROY   You'll text me soon?

ALLISON   I can't. I think I left my phone up on the rocks.

TROY   Ah. Then I know what I'll be doing when I leave here. I'm gonna get your phone.

ALLISON   You hate heights.

160

TROY I will be retrieving your phone and bringing it back to you.

ALLISON You don't have to. I'll get somebody to...oh, God.

TROY What?

ALLISON I was just thinking of the videos I took on that phone. You don't think anybody's been up there, do you? If anybody's found that phone...there is so much shit on that phone...If any of that stuff.... Shit!! Shit!!! Shit!!! Shit!!! The footage of the accident alone...

TROY Don't worry about it. I'll get up there right now, end of story.

ALLISON What am I going to do with you?

TROY I have some good ideas.

ALLISON Go see your girlfriend.

TROY You eat. I'm gonna get that phone. Then I'll go see Courtney. (*He exits.*)

ALLISON Troy!

Notes on the Scene

This scene is fairly straightforward with objectives that are, for the most part, simple and direct. The problem with those straightforward objectives, however, is the fact that they are compromised by strong obstacles that emanate from the given circumstances. For Troy, it's all about Allison (I'll leave the specifics of defining his objectives to you). But how does he get with Allison when his current girlfriend lies in a coma? What kind of person is he if he pursues his true desires? So he has obstacles internally and circumstantially. Whatever Allison may truly want in terms of Troy, she recognizes that this is not the time and place for acting on those feelings. Yet it is obvious that Troy's attempted *siege* (note the title) of her affections is difficult to resist. How do the actors circumnavigate these obstacles, play their objectives, and let the audience know what they are really thinking and feeling without telegraphing it to the other actor as character? This is a big challenge.

In this scene, the two actors must as always play objectives rather than emotions, yet they will need to acknowledge the emotional circumstances of the situation. Their choices must not offend the audience by conveying gross insensitivity or selfishness, yet they must also convey the characters' true feelings for each other. Both actors must rely on what they do physically in order to communicate their affection. How much do these actors as characters need to show each other? How much do they need to reveal to the audience? When do those revelations occur? How do the actors make that happen, when there is not always dialogue to support it? The answers lie in watching each other closely with all their senses and using their business, limited movement, and gestures effectively.

The scene presents some very demanding physical challenges. There is little space to move in, since much of the scene must be played close to each other, probably sitting. The characters are having a very private conversation in a very public place. How do they accomplish this? There is witty banter, humor, and a good deal of topping each other. Troy must use his business to work in conjunction with his dialogue, while Allison must pick up on the messages contained in the way Troy executes his business. There is, of course, a good deal of business for the actor playing Troy to work with, but Allison has few such tools available for her to use. She must tell her story by listening and reacting, much of it with her body. Though the stakes of this scene are not life and death by objective standards, for the characters and actors playing those characters, it must seem as if they are.

CHAPTER TEN

◇◇◇

Scene 3: Quarries

Issues You Will Need to Consider:

High stakes
Strong conflict and objectives
Physical activity and business
Reacting through physicality as well as dialogue
Movement from place to place and physical contact
Story through physical action
Argument
Physical action colors dialogue
Use of wit
Lots of dialogue
Lots of listening and sizing up the other character
Monologue

◇◇◇◇◇◇◇◇◇◇◇◇◇◇◇

Open to JON *just arriving on top of the rock where* COURTNEY *jumped. He has a video camera and is narrating into it.*

JON   So, while the entrance to this section of the quarry is a bit hidden, most of the local kids know about it, and it's a surprisingly easy climb up. There. So, this is the view from the very spot where Courtney jumped. As you can see, it is definitely high up. We can imagine that many have stood on this exact spot, contemplating the jump, but Courtney was the first to actually take the challenge. I will just make my way over to the edge... whoa, it's easy to get dizzy up here. I'm just going to get down on my knees and hold the camera out over the edge, like so. In fact, if I hold the camera in close like this and then thrust it out, that gives us a pretty good simulation of what Courtney might have seen the moment she took the plunge.

(JON *pulls the camera back in to review the footage.* TROY *enters on the platform of rock below* JON. *He is clearly terrified, hugging the rock, not daring to stand at all. He gets down on all fours and starts to look for* ALLISON'*s phone when Jon notices him.*)

JON   Hey!

TROY (*Going flat on his belly.*)   Ah! Jesus Christ!

JON   Hi, how ya doing?

(TROY *rolls onto his back to look up at* JON.)

TROY   Oh, my God, you scared the hell out of me.

JON   Sorry about that. You're Troy, right? You're Courtney's boyfriend.

TROY   Yeah, uh... and you are...?

JON   Jon Blake. Stephanie's brother?

TROY   Oh, yeah. How's it going?

JON   I'm good. What's the matter, you don't like heights?

(TROY *rolls back onto all fours to keep looking for the phone.*)

TROY   That would be an understatement.

JON   What exactly are you doing?

TROY   I'm on a mission.

JON   Uh-huh.

TROY   Looking for a cell phone that got left up here.

JON   You mean that one?

(JON *walks over to the edge to get* ALLISON's *cell.*)

TROY   Yeah, that's the one, thanks. (TROY *scrambles back away from the edge of the cliff, sitting down with his back against the rock wall.*)

JON   I had an uncle who was like, super afraid of heights. And the funny thing is that this guy was very tall. Six foot seven or something. I'm surprised he wasn't wobbly just from life, you know what I mean? I wonder if that's ever happened, someone being so afraid of heights that they can't even stand up.

TROY   That's very funny. I'm not that bad. Um, dude, could you give me that phone?

JON   Is this phone Courtney's?

TROY   No, her friend Allison. She was up here too.

JON   When you said you were on a mission, I assumed it was for Courtney. But you're actually doing something for Allison, right?

TROY   What are you doing up here, anyway?

JON   I'm making a video, a documentary about Courtney's...I don't know what to call it exactly. Jump? Fall? I mean, she did jump, but not the way she wanted to, huh?

TROY   Do you have the family's permission to do this?

JON   To do what?

TROY   You know. Shoot all this stuff.

JON   I don't need their permission. I mean, there are at least five videos of the incident on YouTube already. It's public domain. I'm just gonna mix them all together along with the narration and footage I'm adding. Give the story more context, you know.

TROY   Who are you, Anderson Cooper?

JON   Yeah, right. I wish. No, but I do want to be a journalist or doc maker. I'm trying to establish a web presence.

TROY   That's very cool and all, but I'd really like to get that phone back now.

JON   Tell you what—we can do a trade. I do a brief interview with you, and then you can have Courtney's phone back.

TROY   It's Allison's phone.

JON   Allison's, right. I keep associating you with Courtney, you know.

TROY   Dude, I want to get down from here ASAP.

JON   I completely get it. But this is a great location for an interview. With Courtney's boyfriend. Look, man, I did find the cell for you.

TROY   Okay, okay, but let's make this quick, all right?

JON   Just gotta turn on the camera. There we go. (*Narrating*) Coincidentally, while this reporter was on the scene of the accident, he happened to find Courtney's boyfriend Troy up here as well.

TROY   Hey.

JON   Troy, what was going through your mind when you saw Courtney jump from this height?

TROY   I...

JON   I understand you don't like heights yourself.

TROY   No, I don't.

JON   So that must have made Courtney's leap particularly nerve-wracking for you.

TROY   Actually, I didn't...I was...at work at the time she jumped.

JON   You didn't witness it yourself?

TROY   No. I couldn't be here. I was...working.

JON   Were you in favor of the jump?

TROY   In favor?

JON   Did you encourage Courtney to post the announcement on Facebook that she would be making the attempt?

TROY No, not at all. I didn't.... Look, Courtney does what she does, whether I'm in favor of it or not, whether I even know about it or not.

JON I sense a frustration about that. Do you feel that your girlfriend was reckless?

TROY She took big risks. That's who she is.

JON And how did you feel about that aspect of Courtney's personality? Was her risk-taking part of what attracted you to her?

TROY What?

JON Or was it something you had to tolerate in the relationship?

TROY Okay, shut the camera off, man. Shut it off. What the fuck are you doing?

JON Whaddayou mean?

TROY What the fuck do you care what I tolerated? My relationship with Courtney is none of your fuckin' business.

JON I'm making a documentary, man. This is all important background stuff.

TROY Right.

JON Look, this is all time-sensitive shit. I gotta post it on YouTube right after I edit.

TROY All right. All right. How about we just steer clear of the whole relationship part of things, okay?

JON But that's the main angle here—you're her boyfriend. Nobody else can give us that perspective.

TROY Yeah, I get that, but what attracted me to her and all ... I don't want to go there.

JON You guys are still going out, right?

TROY Yeah, I guess.

JON So what's the problem?

TROY Nothing. Look, can we ... just shift the focus of the questions, okay? And wrap this up.

JON Okay. We're rolling. Now, Troy, you weren't present when Courtney had the accident. You have seen footage, I'm assuming?

TROY Yeah.

JON What was your reaction to it?

TROY Shit—can I say shit?—anyway, God, it was ... awful. I can't believe she survived it. I almost puked. It was horrible ... horrible.

JON You've been to see Courtney at the hospital, right?

TROY Uh, yeah, I've been to the hospital.

JON How does she look?

TROY Look, okay. Enough! That's enough. You said a short interview.

JON Come on, man. Now we're getting into some good shit. If you can just talk about your reaction to seeing Courtney in the hospital ...

TROY I said enough! Now give me the fuckin' phone!

JON   Okay, okay. That line about puking was pretty good. I can definitely use that.

TROY   Great. That's really great. Now, give me . . . (JON *walks over near the edge.*) Dude, give me the fuckin' phone. Now.

JON   Something just occurred to me. This is Allison's phone, right?

TROY   Yeah, so what?

JON   So, this has probably got some really interesting footage on it.

TROY   Give me the phone, man. It's not yours.

JON   It's not yours, either.

TROY (*Picking up a stone*)   Look, man. I'm not good with heights, but I have a decent arm.

JON   If you hit me with that rock, I could easily just, whoops, there goes the phone.

TROY   Don't be a dick. Give me the phone.

JON   Don't you be a dick. Put down the fuckin' rock.

TROY   Look. Allison asked me to come up here and get the phone for her. This is bullshit.

JON   I found the goddamn phone.

TROY   You found it for me. You found it for Allison. Now do the right thing and give it over.

JON   Okay, in a sec. No harm if I just check the video on it first.

TROY   Look, man. Okay, no harm. Just hurry up.

JON   Right. Good, no password protection.

TROY Because we both know that the phone does not belong to you and the video on the phone does not belong to you.

(JON *sets his camera down, sits to watch the video on the phone. Engrossed, he doesn't notice* TROY *crawling toward him.*)

JON Just a sec. Here it is. Oh, now that *is* interesting. Oh, look at that! That is a great angle. She's screaming the whole time, too. Wow.

(TROY *leaps forward, knocking* JON *over.* TROY *grabs the phone from him.*)

JON No, hey! What the hell!

(TROY, *with the phone, scrambles back to his safe spot.*)

TROY What the hell yourself, asshole!

JON You coulda broken my camera!

TROY Your own fault, dick. If you just gave me the phone in the first place.

JON Troy, listen. There is some excellent video on there. People should see it.

TROY (*Picking up the rock again.*) Fuck you.

JON Come on, Troy, why do you have to be like this? I told you, I'm trying to make a documentary. I'm serious.

TROY Yeah, right. And I'm sure your work will do serious honor to Courtney and her family. And serve all mankind with its great insights.

JON It's an important story, man.

TROY   Why? Because it'll get a thousand hits?

JON   What's posted is already getting a ton of traffic. If I put them all together, along with *my* extra footage and what's on *that* phone…

TROY   Then it'll get a million hits. So what?

JON   I'm not going to lie to you. This is important to me. As a journalist. It could help me get into grad school or something.

TROY   I'm out of here.

JON   I have your interview on tape, Troy! It's right here.

TROY   So what?

JON   So…depending on how I edit it, you could either come across as a somewhat caring boyfriend or a total asshole.

TROY   What do you mean? I didn't say anything.

JON   That's just the point. There was a lot of hemming and hawing and shit, and "shut off the cameras" at key moments. You may not come off as much of a hero.

TROY   What? You're trying to blackmail me?

JON   I am trying to make this interaction mutually beneficial. Now, if I could have just a minute with that phone, long enough for me to send the video to my cell, we could *perhaps* re-shoot some of the interview and have it come across as more of a what… valentine?…for Courtney. Or I could obliterate the whole interview entirely; I never saw you up here. Either way…

TROY   All right, listen.

JON I'm listening. (TROY *says nothing for several seconds.*) We can rehearse it if you want or . . .

TROY I . . . if I'm going to come across as a hero to anybody, I want it to be to Allison.

JON Okay.

TROY Not that, I mean, I don't want to look like a jerk about Courtney.

JON Enough said. However you want to play it.

TROY She already knows I'm fighting my fear of heights to be up here.

JON Very noble. I could play that up.

TROY How about if you come across as the bad guy?

JON Reporters can be bad guys, overreaching to get the story.

TROY Exactly. So let's say you were up here first . . .

JON Which I was.

TROY You found the phone and poached the video off of it. Then I showed up.

JON And *you* gallantly wrestled it away from me to return it to your one true love, unaware of my thievery.

TROY Yeah. How would that play?

JON I could make that play extremely well.

TROY Forget about the interview with me—that wouldn't make sense.

JON Absolutely.

TROY This way, I could be protecting Courtney because I didn't want you to have the video and I could look good for risking my life to get Allison's phone back.

JON Win-win. Win-win-win, if you include me.

TROY As long as you can live with your journalistic methods.

JON I don't really see an ethical problem here. This is just a slight timing re-arrangement. It's editing, really.

TROY But how do I know you'll even put all this in your *documentary*?

JON Word of honor.

TROY Sorry, but that's not worth shit.

JON This is a perfect deal. I'll get an excellent story; you'll get an excellent chance to rearrange your romantic situation.

TROY Give me your wallet.

JON What?

TROY Your wallet, with everything in it. And your camera case.

JON Why?

TROY Collateral. Once I see your video posted with me as Allison's hero, then you'll get it back.

JON I can't give you my license. What if I get pulled over?

TROY Drive carefully.

JON I've got a hundred dollars in here.

TROY   The case, too.

JON   And expensive lenses in the case.

TROY   You'll get it all back once you make good on your promise.

JON   I don't know.

TROY   Just like you said—win-win-win. I just need a guarantee.

JON   Okay. It's a deal. Don't lose anything, all right? Here. Give me her phone.

TROY   This never happened, right?

JON   Never. (TROY *hands over the phone. Jon eagerly pulls up the video.*) Nice. Do you want to see this?

TROY   No. I'll wait for the movie to come out.

JON   We push this, then this, then send. Should just take a few seconds.

TROY (*Looking up at the higher platform.*)   God, she was crazy.

JON   You said yourself she was a risk-taker. (*Looking at the phone*) Done. (*Hands back phone*) There you are. Take good care of my equipment, man, and don't spend all my money.

TROY   Wait, wait—don't we need to stage some action?

JON   Like what?

TROY   Like me finding you with the phone, us fighting over it. Shit like that.

JON   I could just talk about what happened.

TROY   I thought a picture was worth a thousand words.

JON   And a video is worth a million. You're right—some shaky camera stuff, you sounding angry, a scuffle. Actually, this'll really up the interest level. I like it.

TROY   But do not get us near the edge.

JON   All right, I need to get a shot of finding it first. Just put it down on the ground, near the edge.

TROY   What?

JON   Just joking. I'll take it.

TROY   You have no idea what it's like.

(JON *sets the cell down near the edge.*)

JON   All right, camera rolling. (*To* TROY) Don't say anything—you haven't arrived on the scene yet.

TROY   Got it.

JON (*Narrating for the camera*)   And now I'm on the part of the rocks where Courtney's friend was watching her. Hey, what's this? A phone? I can't believe it. I think Courtney's friend must have left her phone up here. I wonder if, by any chance, she might have...there's a video on here with the right date! There is video on the phone of Courtney's jump! What are the chances? All right, that should do it. (*To* TROY) Now, let's get some of us fighting.

TROY   What do you want me to do?

JON   I'm going to put the camera down here, filming, like you knocked it out of my hand—it'll just show our feet and stuff. The main thing is, it'll pick up your voice.

TROY   So what should we do?

JON   Okay, you come at me yelling about the phone. Like what you did earlier when you got it from me.

TROY   Stay away from the edge.

JON   Okay, okay, go!

TROY   Give me that phone, man! It's not yours! You're not getting the video off it!

(JON *keeps the phone from* TROY, *making the struggle more intense than it needs to be.*)

JON   No, no, it's not yours, either.

TROY   Hand it over. Allison told me to get it for her! Give me that damned...

JON   No way! No! I found it!

(*In the struggle, the phone gets knocked from* JON's *hand and falls off the edge.*)

TROY   No! Fuck, what did you do?

JON   Uh-oh.

TROY   You moron! You complete asshole! Why did you do that?

JON   I didn't do it! It just happened!

TROY   You were supposed to hold on to it!

JON   I'm sorry. You're stronger than I am. I couldn't help it.

TROY   I cannot believe this. Fuck!

JON   No worries. We've got the footage. She'll know you tried to get the phone. She'll still be extremely grateful.

TROY (*Grabbing the wallet and the camera bag*)   You're not getting this back until I see it online! And it better be good!

JON   It'll be up tomorrow, don't you worry.

TROY   Tonight! (*With a final glance toward where the phone dropped.*) Shit!

(TROY *exits.* JON *takes out his phone, pushes a button to retrieve the video he sent to it, and smiles while he watches.*)

JON   Exclusive. Perfect.

Notes on the Scene

Quarries," of course, is a pun on the two meanings of the word. The scene, like the first in the collection, takes place in a quarry, and in this one, the characters circle around each other as though each was the quarry of the other. The stakes are high because of the inherent danger in the environment, especially for Troy, but these characters become so adversarial that they pose a threat to each other as well. The objectives in the etude are simple and clear for each of the characters, and the tactics they use are based almost totally on the give-and-take of the strategic game they are playing. Listening and reacting moment by moment, and playing the discoveries, new information, wins, and losses, will be crucial if the scene is to be believable, clear, and compelling. Actors will also have a wonderful opportunity to craft memorable moments by executing clear tactical shifts following each beat ending

The dialogue and physical action in the scene blend seamlessly, challenging the actor to integrate movement, business, and gesture with the snappy one-upping in the dialogue. The testosterone is palpable in this scene, and the actors playing Troy and Jon will need to turn on their "butch" to make it work. The wins, losses, and discoveries are substantial, so the actors will have many opportunities to tell their moment-to-moment stories through what they do physically in those transitional sequences.

The physicality of the setting is worth noting as well. Troy's progress across rocks and ledges that terrify him will be an ongoing activity that he must negotiate while trying to deal with Jon. The actors will need to use their imaginations to create a set that will help them to produce the required illusion. There are also a camera, phone, and physical struggles with each other, both staged and real, that the actors must choreograph. The actor playing Jon has the opportunity to actually make us believe he is shooting footage for his documentary while moving through the environment even as he provides impromptu narration. How should doing that sound? As an audience we'd recognize a truthful delivery, but can the actor create it? In short, any actor looking for a scene to challenge or develop his physical acting while handling dialogue will find plenty to work with here.

There are a few other tricky elements to be found in this scene as well. How does an on-camera interview sound? How should Troy sound while being interviewed? How does he show his discomfort? How do the characters believably handle the arc that leads up to Troy's Neanderthal threat with a rock? Or the arc in the interview questions that lead to Troy's blow-up? How does someone react to the threat of blackmail? What does Jon see and hear when he plays back Allison's cell phone? Can the actors as characters make us believe that they really lose the phone during their fake struggle—and that all of this is taking place high atop a dangerous cliff? A challenge to any actor!

◇◇

CHAPTER ELEVEN

Scene 4:
Best Buy Ethics

Issues You Will Need to Consider:

Argument or discussion of an issue
Simple, clear-cut, cause-and-effect sequence
Urgency not necessarily obvious in situation
Strong conflict and objectives
Clear and varied tactics
Limited physical activity
Business and movement need to be invented
Use of wit
Personal information must be handled
Monologues

◇◇◇◇◇◇◇◇◇◇◇◇◇◇◇◇◇◇

The video section of a store such as Best Buy. JON *is looking at a display when* ANNA, *who works there, approaches him.*

ANNA   Hi, are you finding everything you need?

JON   I don't know. I was looking for a sixteen-gig memory card.

ANNA   Sixteen, sixteen—here's an eight.

JON   Yeah, too small.

ANNA   I see here where they're supposed to be, but it looks like we're out. We should be getting some more in on Tuesday.

JON   I'll check Circuit City.

ANNA   Oops, didn't hear that. Competition. But just between you and me, that's where I get mine.

JON   You look really familiar. (ANNA *gives him a look.*) No, it's not a pickup line. You honestly do look familiar. You're from around here, right?

ANNA   Yes. This is still sounding like a pickup line.

JON   No, swear to God. I know you. Drives me crazy when I can't place a face. It'll keep me awake tonight.

ANNA   So, it's not a pickup line, but now you're claiming I'm going to keep you up tonight, huh?

JON   Okay, I give! I will slink away now.

ANNA   I'm just pulling your chain. I graduated from Clearview.

JON   Hm. I'm still not making the connection.

ANNA   Let me guess—you want my cell number so, when you do wake up in the middle of the night and make the connection, you can let me know.

JON   Funny.

ANNA   No?

JON   I would wait until the morning.

ANNA   Ah, a gentleman.

JON   Through and through.

ANNA   Oops, there's the manager. (*Show for the boss*) So, if you'd like me to order a sixteen-gigabyte memory card, I'd be happy to do that for you.

JON   No, you say they'll be in on Tuesday, right? I can come back then.

ANNA   Okay.

JON   In the meantime, could you tell me a little about...?

ANNA   Coast is clear. Thanks.

JON   No problem. You're not planning to go to a college out west, are you? Maybe I saw you at the college fair.

ANNA   Nope. Staying local. What're you studying?

JON   Journalism. Going to Utah State.

ANNA   Cool. So, listen, I should probably...

JON   Yeah, yeah, no worries. If I figure out where I know you from, I'll call the store.

ANNA   Or...you could always stop back in.

JON   Maybe I'll do that.

ANNA   Journalism, huh? That's a pretty tough field.

JON   Yeah, but I love it. Do what you love and you'll never work a day in your life.

ANNA   But you might never get paid a day in your life.

JON   Touché. You should check out my stuff online.

ANNA   Oh, now we're really getting into pickup lines.

JON   No, no—I do some journalism already. I've put together a few stories. Check out VidJon 1489 on YouTube. Subscribe to me, if you want.

ANNA   You're VidJon 1489?

JON   Yeah. You've seen my stuff?

ANNA   I saw that...thing...you slapped together about Courtney.

JON   My documentary.

ANNA   That what you call it?

JON   Yeah. What would you call it?

ANNA   Trash maybe. Garbage. Some low-life shit.

JON   Wow. Liked it, huh?

ANNA   Yeah. See, Courtney's a good friend of mine.

JON   Oh! Yeah, got it now. You were there in the crowd when she jumped. I was right behind you.

ANNA   Yeah, I was there.

JON   Okay—now I can sleep.

ANNA That's too bad. Courtney's a really good friend. I know her family and everything.

JON How're they doing?

ANNA Oh, like you care. You're a fuckin' asshole, you know that? In case it never occurred to you, this has been pretty hard on them.

JON I bet.

ANNA So you're Jon, right?

JON Jon Blake. And I can see from your name tag that you are Anna.

ANNA (*Pulling up nose to nose*) The thing is, *Jon*, I respect your right to post whatever you want on Facebook and YouTube...

JON Is your manager gonna come back? Don't want you to get in trouble.

ANNA Don't worry about it. He makes his rounds about once an hour, then drinks coffee in the back room the rest of the time.

JON Ah. Then most of the time you're free to be you, right?

ANNA Yeah. Like I was saying, I know it's your right to make your videos...

JON Most of the footage was already out there, you know. I just compiled it, edited it, added some narration.

ANNA Yeah. And then you took the video from Allison's phone, which you didn't have permission to use.

JON Not technically, no, but I did find the phone in a public place. It's a gray area.

ANNA   Look, let me tell you something. Courtney's parents have been at the hospital since this thing happened. But it's only a matter of time before they find out that there's video out there...that is, if they don't know already. And your... documentary...if that's what you're calling it...

JON   That's what it is.

ANNA   Your *documentary* is, like, a one-stop shop for people to see all the gory details.

JON   And to get a sense of the place and the circumstances. I tried to provide context.

ANNA   Yeah, right. Well, no matter what service you think you're providing, your video will kill Court's parents when they see it.

JON   Is that right?

ANNA   That's not journalism. That's some kind of voyeuristic bullshit.

JON   Two points. What happened to Courtney is a compelling story, so I do think it's news and, frankly, the line between news and entertainment has always been extremely blurry.

ANNA   But Courtney didn't hurt herself to entertain people or to be a news story.

JON   Yeah, then why was she up there?

ANNA   She wanted to...

JON   Sounds like she wanted to be entertaining to me.

ANNA   You know what half the comments were about, don't you?

JON State of the world. I don't control what people...

ANNA No, but you have control over what you choose to post, asshole! It was yours to put up and it's yours to take down.

JON True.

ANNA And I'm asking you, please, to take it down. As Courtney's friend, I'm asking you to take it down. Please.

JON I hear you. The truth is, I got a note from one of my future professors at Utah State. He liked the story.

ANNA But what about the part where she shows her breasts? Did your professor like that? How is that good reporting?

JON I fuzzed it out.

ANNA Only because YouTube would've taken it down if you hadn't.

JON True, but also because her tiny breasts were not the issue.

(*She slaps him.*)

JON The minute she got up there... no... the minute she announced to the world she was going to make that jump, she was no longer innocent. She chose to climb up there to a clearly dangerous spot —because she wanted to. She wanted an audience. That wasn't an innocent move, I hate to tell you. And now, if you don't mind, I'm going to go look for my sixteen-gig memory card elsewhere, thank you very much.

ANNA Wait, I've got a news story for you, Mr. Hotshot Journalist. How about this? You go to a party with your camera. Your friend says, "Hey, stand by. That girl just dropped a pill I gave her. You oughta make a movie of this."

189

JON I wouldn't shoot that.

ANNA It's compelling. It's entertaining, right? It's news. She strips and lets guys grope her and gets completely degraded...hell, you could just fuzz out anything that wouldn't make it on YouTube. What's more compelling than watching some slurring, stumbling chick get tossed around by a bunch of guys, right?

JON That is a ridiculous comparison.

ANNA Yeah, why?

JON First, the girl was not in control. She was not making a choice.

ANNA It was her choice to take the pill.

JON Yeah, but she didn't know what she was taking.

ANNA What difference does it make?

JON There's a line.

ANNA And where's that line, huh? Where exactly does it get crossed? Because somebody behind the camera could say, "Hey, she's at a party, she took that pill—she knew what she was doing. I'm just making a public service video here, showing what could happen." Or does the line get crossed when the girl wakes up and finds out she's been plastered all over the Internet? Or maybe the line gets crossed when she sees the comments on Facebook, or whispered behind her back, or even said to her face? Does the line get crossed when some ignorant jerks start calling her a whore? Tell me where the fuckin' line is. I'd really like to know.

JON Look...

ANNA   Or maybe the line doesn't get crossed until she starts believing what people are saying about her? When she can't take living with herself anymore and decides to swallow a bottle of her mother's sleeping pills?

JON   Hey, come on.

ANNA   Come on what?

JON   Look, I'm sorry if some bad stuff has happened to you, but...

ANNA   I wasn't talking about me.

JON   Whoever you were talking about—a "friend." Whoever. I'm sorry if that happened to somebody you know. Whoever did that was completely out of line.

ANNA   Unlike you, who is completely justified.

JON   My conscience is clear.

ANNA   Then how about this: Courtney is my friend. I love her. You're hurting me... and a lot of other very nice people... by leaving up your video. Please take it down.

JON   I appreciate what you're saying...

ANNA   Please take it down.

JON   Your manager is back. He's looking.

ANNA   I don't care. Please, Jon.

JON   I'll think about it. I'll think about it.

(*He exits.* ANNA *watches him leave as the scene ends.*)

◇◇

Notes on the Scene

◇◇◇◇◇◇◇◇◇◇◇◇◇◇◇

Unlike the previous three scenes, this one is mostly a debate over ethics. The argument, as it plays out, is a matter of opinion, and for the most part, the actors as characters must focus on trying to change each other's mind. Though the objectives are strong and clear, the tactics for much of the scene are based on the intelligence of the argument rather than on any kind of subtext. Toward the end of the scene, Anna shifts her tactics to the more personal and emotional, but that strategy comes out of her desperation to find a way to keep Jon from going ahead with his plan. The biggest challenge in the scene, then, is in finding the humanity in the situation and in the characters while making the argument. The scene must seem more than the dialectic about journalistic ethics that it is in reality.

There are good arguments to be made on both sides of the question being debated, and the actors must make them effectively, landing the wins, losses, and discoveries. The scene has a terrific arc, and the actors must find the stepping-stones that make for the big moments as they progress from initial attraction to nuclear war. They must also decide what the end of that arc will look like. Where exactly is Jon in terms of the argument when he leaves? Is he softening? Will he be considering Anna's appeal, or is he just appeasing her to get on with his life? What choices make for the best story? Would your answer be the same if the scene were being done in isolation as it would be if you were approaching it in the context of the entire play? Explain.

One of the questions that the actors playing these characters must consider is whether the audience should like them and want them to get together. At the top of the scene, there seems to be an attraction. Should the audience be rooting for this to progress? How does the audience feel about Jon? Clearly, if the actors approach this scene as an independent entity, then the actor playing Jon can easily create an initial charm. But if this scene is approached in the context of the overall play, that actor will face a much harder task. Even then, however, Anna must see something in Jon that makes her attracted to him, at least until the big reveal.

Other challenges in this scene include finding the stakes, making choices about having a private conversation in a public place, and finding a body of physical choices that makes the scene seem more than two people standing in space having a debate. The stakes here are not literally life and death, so the actors must find the stakes and personal urgency to make them seem so, if the scene is to take off. Once the stakes and urgency are found, how can two people standing in a Best Buy maintain the urgency and not draw undue attention to themselves and each other? What does a private argument look and sound like in a public place? And what things can the actors physically do that will make the scene seem more than a political debate?

The answer to the last question lies in coming up with things employees and customers can do in an electronics store. Finding ways to integrate business with the argument on a semi-bare set will be a challenge. Space, movement and business are the ingredients actors will have to use effectively if the scene is going to be truly believable and interesting.

◇◇◇

CHAPTER TWELVE

Scene 5:
The Power of Myth

Issues You Will Need to Consider:

Strong objectives
Urgency not obvious
Tactics
Wins, losses, and discoveries
Non-climactic on paper
Constant reacting
Business and changing activity
Movement in limited space
Argument and discussion of issue
Mix of dialogue and business
Personal information and lists
Monologues

◇◇◇◇◇◇◇◇◇◇◇◇◇◇◇◇◇

ANNA *intently typing on her computer. Her sister* IZZY *enters, holding a sketchbook and some pencils.*

IZZY   What are you working on?

ANNA   Oh, hi, uh, nothing. Just…checking e-mail. (*She closes the computer.*) All done. What about you?

IZZY   Looking for a good place to draw.

ANNA   This is a good spot, right here. Nice and bright. Sit down.

IZZY   You know, you don't have to shut down every time you hear me coming.

ANNA   I know. I wasn't.

IZZY   Right. I actually used my cell phone today. I sent a text and got an answer.

ANNA   Wow. That's…good.

IZZY   So, what were you reading? You were looking pretty intense when I came in.

ANNA   Nah, nothing important.

IZZY   You were really pounding on those keys.

ANNA   Just habit, I guess. What are you drawing?

IZZY   A little art therapy, that's all. I did a lot of that in the hospital. I liked it.

ANNA   Good. Can I see?

IZZY   Not really for public consumption.

ANNA   Okay.

IZZY But hey, you're not public; you're my sister. (IZZY *hands the sketchpad to* ANNA.) Just don't hate me because I'm so damned talented.

ANNA (*Flipping through the sketch pad.*) Whooo.

IZZY Yeah, I know. Those are from my dark and angry period.

ANNA Yeah.

IZZY And so are those.

ANNA This one's not so dark.

IZZY Yeah. I didn't draw that. I asked the kid next to me if she wanted to contribute to my portfolio. I felt it needed diversity.

ANNA Nice touch.

IZZY I'll let her know you thought so. If she's not dead. She was in for multiple attempts. That's the latest one I'm working on, that page there.

ANNA Uh...

IZZY What do you think?

ANNA I think it's...pretty blank.

IZZY You're kidding. You don't see the snow-white bird rising into the blinding white sky?

ANNA No...not really. Well, maybe I do. Sorta.

IZZY Yeah, well, look closely.

ANNA You pulling my leg?

IZZY No, it's there. Shit!

ANNA Oh, yeah. I think I see it now. Right. (IZZY *stares at* ANNA *for a long moment.*) What's the matter?

IZZY Nothing. (*Pause*) Can you do me a favor?

ANNA Sure. What do you need?

IZZY I need for you to get the "f" out of this room.

ANNA Huh?

IZZY Get out, okay? I don't want you in here.

ANNA (*Rising, taking her computer.*) Okay. Sure, Iz. Whatever you...

IZZY Why are you taking the computer?

ANNA I don't know; I'm just...

IZZY Just leave it, okay?

ANNA Leave it?

IZZY What's the matter? You don't trust me with it?

ANNA No, it's fine. I'll leave it.

IZZY If you don't trust me just take it, okay?

ANNA No, I'll leave it.

IZZY Suit yourself. Now go.

ANNA Did I do something?

IZZY I said leave!

ANNA Okay, no problem.

IZZY Could you get me a drink?

ANNA   What? A drink? Sure. What do you want?

IZZY   Surprise me.

ANNA   Okay. Be right back.

(ANNA *exits.* IZZY *watches her leave, then turns to a page in her note-book and starts to draw.* ANNA *returns with a half-full soda bottle and a glass. She sets the glass next to* IZZY *and pours the soda into it.*)

IZZY   What's this?

ANNA   You wanted a drink.

IZZY   What is it?

ANNA   Diet Sprite.

IZZY   No ice?

ANNA   Do you want ice?

IZZY   I always take ice.

ANNA   I'll get you ice.

IZZY   Forget it.

ANNA   I can get you ice.

IZZY   I said forget it.

ANNA   Okay.

(ANNA *turns to exit.*)

IZZY   Where are you going?

ANNA   I thought you said you wanted to be alone.

IZZY   Why? Are you afraid to stay in the same room with me?

ANNA   No, I can. Do you want to talk, or...

IZZY   No. Just be here, okay?

ANNA   Sure. Absolutely.

(IZZY *goes back to drawing.* ANNA *opens her computer.*)

IZZY   I thought you were done with that.

ANNA   Is it bothering you?

IZZY   I thought you said you were done.

ANNA   I was just going to...

IZZY   Anna, listen to me. I have to tell you something really important.

ANNA   Okay. Go ahead.

IZZY   I'm going to pull my pants down now, and you need kiss my ass.

ANNA   What...?

IZZY   You need to kiss my fat ass.

ANNA   Your ass is not fat.

ANNA   Whatever. Those are doctor's orders. Whenever I feel the need to have my ass kissed, I am supposed to ask.

ANNA   I...don't follow you.

(IZZY *starts to laugh.* ANNA *looks puzzled, then laughs, too, but tentatively.*)

IZZY   I've been messing with your head, Anna.

ANNA What?

IZZY I've been testing you. And you failed, really bad.

ANNA I don't get it.

(IZZY *turns to the blank page in her notebook.*)

IZZY What is this?

ANNA It's your snow-white dove rising into a blinding...

IZZY No, it's a fucking blank piece of paper. It's a variation on the old polar bear in a snowstorm joke.

ANNA Oh. I sorta thought that.

IZZY And when I told you to leave the room when you were here first, and it's your room, that was me being fucking rude.

ANNA I just thought you needed...

IZZY That was fucking rude, Anna. You know what rude is?

ANNA What is your point?

IZZY Look, I need my sister.

ANNA I'm here.

IZZY No, I need *my* sister, not some robot trained to handle fragile things. Do you get me?

ANNA I get you. But it's not easy, you know. We almost lost you.

IZZY I understand that. And I'm sorry. But it's lonely, stuck here behind the fragile sign.

ANNA   I understand. I'm sorry. I'm really sorry. I just don't always know how to act.

IZZY   So just be yourself, okay?

ANNA   Okay.

IZZY   So now, will you please get me some ice for this lame, warm, flat soda you brought me?

ANNA   You've got legs. Get your own fuckin' ice.

IZZY   Better. Thank you.

ANNA   Kiss *my* fat ass.

IZZY   Your ass is not...well,...

(*They both laugh.*)

IZZY   Now this *is* a test. What were you working on when I came in here?

ANNA   I don't know.

IZZY   I said this is a test.

ANNA   Okay. I guess you're gonna find out sooner or later.

IZZY   What?

ANNA   Courtney Matheson is in the hospital. She's in a coma.

IZZY   No! What the hell happened?

ANNA   She tried to jump from that spot in the quarry.

IZZY   You're kidding.

ANNA   She...miscalculated and...it was bad.

IZZY When?

ANNA A week ago.

IZZY A week ago. Oh, God. Courtney. So she was there in the hospital the same time I was?

ANNA Yeah.

IZZY And nobody told me.

ANNA Come on. You had plenty to deal with. You still have *plenty* to deal with. I probably shouldn't have told you. We all decided...

IZZY That I couldn't handle it?

ANNA There's more to it than just her accident.

IZZY Keep talking.

ANNA Izzy...

IZZY Anna, you need to tell me. I'm not a china doll. Don't make me feel crazier than I am.

ANNA Everybody took video of Allison's jump, on their cell phones. No one thought she'd get hurt.

IZZY Let me guess. It's gone viral.

ANNA Most people didn't post theirs, thank God. But this one A H—VidJon 1489—thinks he's this big-time journalist, right? And he not only compiles all the videos out there into one, but he finds Allison's phone at the quarry, and steals her up-close stuff and adds it to the piece of crap he's calling a documentary.

IZZY And he won't take it down.

ANNA Uh-uh. He came into the store. I asked him myself. The shit. I ended up slapping him.

IZZY You slapped him? He was a customer, and you slapped him. Did you get fired?

ANNA No, but I wouldn't care if I did.

IZZY That's weird. I'm the one who does things like that.

ANNA He really pissed me off.

IZZY Because of what happened with me.

ANNA I guess.

IZZY So what were you doing when I came in just now?

ANNA Commenting on his stupid video. Trying to make people see what an irresponsible asshole he is.

IZZY But the damage is already done, right?

ANNA Yeah, it is. But still, he had no right.

IZZY That's the way people are, I guess.

ANNA They weren't always this way.

IZZY Maybe. Show me his video.

ANNA No way, Iz. That's a bad idea.

IZZY I'm gonna see it eventually. You know that.

ANNA Not now, though. It's too soon.

IZZY I'd rather watch it with you than alone in my room. You know I'm not gonna be able to stop myself.

ANNA Yeah, I know. Fuck Facebook. Fuck YouTube. Fuck cell phones.

IZZY You can't change what is. I heard that enough in the hospital. It won't break me, Anna, promise.

(ANNA *sighs heavily and opens her computer, pulling up the video.*)

ANNA At least let me turn off the sound. I don't want to listen to Jon's idiot commentary.

IZZY Okay. (*They watch.*) God, that is crazy high.

ANNA Nobody's ever jumped from there.

IZZY Figures Courtney would be the one to try. Look at her up there. God!

ANNA (*Averting her eyes.*) I can't watch it again.

(IZZY *watches, grimacing.*)

IZZY Oh, shit.

ANNA I told you.

(IZZY *pauses the video.*)

IZZY She survived that; I can't believe it. What are the doctors saying?

ANNA Everybody's trying to stay hopeful. She broke a bunch of bones, including her back.

IZZY Christ.

ANNA But coming out of the coma—that's the first hurdle that needs jumping. How ya doing?

IZZY   What do you mean?

ANNA   Watching the video.

IZZY   You mean did it push me over the edge? Am I going to go find some more pills to swallow?

ANNA   Yeah, that is exactly what I mean. You wanted real, Iz. That's what's on everybody's mind. Are you gonna try to off yourself again? Is something gonna set you off—some comment, some soda without ice, some video I never showed you? We're scared, Iz!

IZZY   Look. What you just did—telling me how you actually feel, talking to me about Courtney, letting me watch the video, treating me like I'm not a piece of blown glass—that is what's going to get me better. Okay?

ANNA   Okay. (*Pause*) Do me a favor, though. If you're thinking of framing any of your works of art for my birthday…don't. Go with the gift card instead.

(*They laugh.*)

IZZY   It's a deal. (*Pause*) You know what watching that video reminded me of?

ANNA   *The Children's Illustrated Book of Greek Myths* Mom used to read to us.

IZZY   Wow! Same wavelength or what?

ANNA   Big falls from great heights stick with you, I guess.

IZZY   Yeah. Courtney jumping off the cliff—Icarus…

ANNA   Wings of wax. . .

IZZY Melting in the sun. Cause he tried to fly too high.

ANNA Too much pride.

IZZY Greek news story and we're still talking about his flight. Courtney's lucky in a way, you know?

ANNA How's that?

IZZY At least she's famous for trying to do something cool, something sort of… grand, you know? I just get to go down in Internet history under the title "Drunk Party Slut."

ANNA Izzy.

IZZY Remember at that sleepover, when Courtney kept texting those pictures to Troy?

ANNA Yeah.

IZZY That was so funny. She was so cool, doing that. She didn't care, you know, just whipped out the camera and psh, cleavage shot; psh, thigh shot; psh, crotch shot.

ANNA That's Courtney.

IZZY So smooth, you know? Troy just called her. She lured him right in. Total control. Best lookin' guy in the senior class! With a crotch shot! The night of the party…

ANNA Are we still talking about Allison's?

IZZY No, *the* party. At Robbie's.

ANNA Izzy.

IZZY Courtney was still in my head, I guess. I told Nick, "Get the good stuff." He's always has his cell phone out, shooting everything. I wanted him on me all the time. I sorta knew what I was doing. I wanted Courtney's power. I wanted the attention. I told Nick, no matter what, if I got trashed or whatever, he should...keep the camera on me. He should get the good stuff. I guess that's what he did, huh?

ANNA Hmm.

IZZY I saw you there, you know.

ANNA No, I didn't know.

IZZY You shouldn't have left me.

ANNA You think? You think this is the first time that occurred to me? You think I never thought about the fact that I left my little sister at a party where she was obviously out of her mind? But I didn't want to make a scene. So I left. Didn't want to take away your fifteen minutes.

IZZY You shouldn't have left me.

ANNA I realize that now. But then...well, I just didn't want to take away your fifteen minutes.

IZZY You're right, I wanted that. People talking about me. Like they talk about Courtney. It's what everybody wants, right? To be the focus of attention. Icarus flying toward the sun.

ANNA Yeah.

IZZY I should have known that moron Nick would follow my instructions to the letter. (*She takes the empty bottle of soda and screws the cap back on.*) Spin the bottle?

ANNA What?

IZZY Well, we're both feeling guilty as shit. Let's let the bottle say who's more to blame. Take the responsibility out of our hands.

ANNA You mean like leave it to the gods?

IZZY Exactly. Let's leave it to the gods to punish us.

ANNA Spin it.

IZZY You spin it.

(*The lights fade.*)

◇◇◇

Notes on the Scene

◇◇◇◇◇◇◇◇◇◇◇◇◇◇◇◇

This is another scene where the stakes and urgency are not apparent at first, but both Izzy and Anna are playing objectives that must be masked carefully with well-chosen tactics. Each dances around the other, trying to avoid an outbreak of hostility. The backstory and emotional circumstances, whether the actors are considering the whole play or simply piecing together imaginary circumstances to justify the actions of the scene, fuel everything each of the actors as character does and says. In other words, the stakes are actually extremely high, but they must be hidden until the script demands that they be revealed. Deciding where and how that happens is the big challenge in solving the scene.

This scene requires a lot of listening and reacting, but the characters must keep from showing the whole truth until everything is out in the open. Yet the audience must believe when the genie is out of the box that the characters were picking up on more than they let on. Anna's willingness to take Izzy's abuse must be tempered with signs that she is not oblivious to how she is being treated. Izzy must see that how she is treating Anna is having an effect on her sister. Finding ways of show this and making the arc toward the explosion must be accomplished through the physical action of the scene and the way the dialogue is delivered.

Business, gesture, and movement in the limited space dictated by the scene will force the actors to be very specific about how they execute all this physicality—sketching, looking at the computer, going and coming from the room, etc. In addition, the way the sisters physically interact in order to show alienation and ultimately, love, will be as important to the storytelling as the dialogue.

The dialogue offers some wonderful challenges as well. The heart-felt monologues, filled with emotion yet clearly aimed at fulfilling objectives, will give the actors an opportunity to craft their moments as well as be inspired by them. The arc of understanding in the characters when they listen to these monologues will be equally challenging. In the end, this is a very emotional scene. How can the actors communicate all that emotion through their actions?

And finally, what is "The Power of Myth," and how does it relate to the actions and meaning of this scene?

◇◇◇◇◇◇◇◇◇◇◇◇◇◇◇◇◇◇◇◇◇◇◇◇◇◇◇◇◇◇◇◇◇

CHAPTER THIRTEEN

Scene 6: Tapeworms and Memory Cards

Issues You Will Need to Consider:

Strong conflict and objectives

Life-and-death stakes

Cause-and-effect scene

Business and physicality

Physical contact

Storytelling through physicality

Physical action colors dialogue

Physical actions requiring attention of other character

Listening with all senses required

Big arc to scene

Wit, punch lines

Personal information and lists

Large amount of dialogue

Monologues

◇◇◇◇◇◇◇◇◇◇◇◇◇◇

We discover IZZY *on the lower ledge of the cliff, lying on her stomach, dropping stones over the edge. It is night. A candle sits beside* IZZY's *head. She has the soda bottle with her, too, and her notebook. After a moment,* IZZY *sits up and spins the bottle. When it stops, she mumbles to herself about where it landed, then marks a tally in her notebook. She spins it twice more, marking the result each time.* JACKIE *enters.*

JACKIE   Iz.

IZZY (*Startled*)   Whoa, shit! Cousin Jackie. Hello, Cousin Jackie.

JACKIE   People are looking for you.

IZZY   People have found me. Cousin Jackie is people.

JACKIE   You been drinking a little, Iz?

IZZY   That would not be smart for someone in my condition.

JACKIE   And what condition is that?

IZZY   Delicate.

JACKIE   Are you in a delicate condition?

IZZY   Not that kind. I decided to light a candle. I decided to hold a little—virgil. That's not right.

JACKIE   Come on, let's get going.

IZZY   What am I holding? It's not a virgil.

JACKIE   Vigil.

IZZY   Vigil, right, in honor of Courtney.

JACKIE   She woke up, you know.

IZZY   She did? That's great. Wow! See, my virgil worked. My candle is magic. It wouldn't stay lit, but still, it's magic.

JACKIE   I put your bike in the back of my truck, Iz.

IZZY   You did?

JACKIE   Yeah. You left it on the side of the road.

IZZY   I did?

JACKIE   Yeah. That's how I found you.

IZZY   You did?

JACKIE   You are drunk, aren't you? Also a bit sarcastic, no?

IZZY   Breathalyze me. If I get higher than a .10 sarcasm level, lock me up.

JACKIE   Let's get going.

IZZY   Where do we want to get going to, Cousin Jackie?

JACKIE   I'm taking you home. It's late.

IZZY   Did you see her?

JACKIE   Who?

IZZY   Courtney. Did you see her jump?

JACKIE   No.

IZZY   Did you watch the video?

JACKIE   No.

IZZY   Did you watch mine? Drunk Party Slut?

(JACKIE *does not answer.*)

IZZY You did!

JACKIE Look. Your parents are worried. It's late, and I've got better things to do than...

IZZY Did you go see Courtney in the hospital?

JACKIE No.

IZZY Me either. I was there, when she was, you know. We were practically roommates, but I didn't see her. I thought about her a lot, though. Still am. She's awake, huh?

JACKIE Yeah. Woke up this afternoon.

IZZY She gonna be all right?

JACKIE She's awake. That's about all anybody knows at this point. Isabelle, we can have this conversation in the truck. I want to go home.

IZZY I know what she did wrong.

JACKIE In the truck, Iz—come on!

IZZY I studied the clips. Watched 'em over and over. She pushed too hard. Gotta stay cool. When you're up in the clouds.

JACKIE What?

IZZY I said when you're up in the clouds. You know... *flying toward* the *sun.*

JACKIE Christ, you are drunk. (JACKIE *goes to* IZZY *and tries to lift her up.*) Let's go.

(IZZY *playfully backs away from* JACKIE, *getting near the edge.*)

JACKIE   Careful! Jesus! Come away from there, would you?

IZZY   I'm being a pain in the ass, aren't I?

JACKIE   You are definitely being a pain in *my* ass.

IZZY   Okay. Let's get going. I'll leave the candle. It wouldn't stay lit. I needed one of those ones you put in the cake, you know? You blow and blow and it won't go out. I think somebody did that to me once. I think there's a video of that somewhere, when I was a little kid, blowing and blowing on that candle. I'm surprised somebody didn't post it. How come people are always catching me doing stupid stuff on camera? Blowing candles and other shit like that.

JACKIE   How about sometime this week, huh? It's cold.

IZZY   Do me a favor?

JACKIE   I did you a favor. I found you. Now do me a favor. Get your ass up and let's go.

IZZY   Cousin Jackie, always taking care of us.

JACKIE   Yeah.

IZZY   How come you got to babysit us when you were only, like, two years older?

JACKIE   Because I was about ten years more mature. Still am. Get up.

IZZY   Do me a favor?

JACKIE   I'm about ready to drop kick your ass off that cliff.

215

IZZY Spin the bottle for me.

JACKIE What are you talking about?

IZZY I've spun it almost a thousand times. See? I've kept track in my notebook. 337 times it's pointed that way (*She points toward the quarry below.*), 318 times it's pointed that way (*She points toward solid ground.*), 362 times it's pointed to God. That's what I call it if it doesn't point to the quarry or back up there.

JACKIE That's a thousand seventeen, Iz.

IZZY Really?

JACKIE You've spun that thing a thousand seventeen times.

IZZY You did that in your head?

JACKIE You know what that is, spinning that bottle a thousand seventeen times?

(JACKIE *kicks the bottle off the edge.*) That's fucked up, Isabelle.

IZZY Hey!

JACKIE Let's go, goddamn it!

IZZY That was my chooser!

JACKIE Yeah, and this is your magic candle. (*She throws it over the edge.*) Bye-bye.

IZZY You're such a bully! What did you do that for?

(JACKIE *grabs the notebook.*)

JACKIE How 'bout this?

IZZY Do not throw that over the edge, Jackie!

216

JACKIE   Then you better start walking in the next ten seconds. I'm done with this shit, okay?

IZZY   You're supposed to treat me better than that, you know. I tried to kill myself.

JACKIE   Boo-hoo, Izzy. You didn't, though, did you?

IZZY   You would've been glad if I did, huh?

JACKIE   No, 'cause then I would've had to miss a whole day of work for your funeral.

IZZY   Why do you hate me?

JACKIE   If I hated you, I would've said tough shit when your mother called, and just watched the rest of *American Idol*. Instead, I got in my truck and drove around for the last three fucking hours looking for you.

IZZY   Are you glad you found me?

JACKIE   Yeah, Iz, I'm glad.

IZZY   Why wouldn't you spin my bottle?

JACKIE   For the same reason I put your pacifier down the garbage disposal when you were six. You don't need it. Now for God's sake, can we go?

IZZY   It is chilly up here.

JACKIE   Glad you noticed.

(JACKIE *turns to leave.* IZZY *follows at first, then begins to climb up to the higher level of the cliff.* JACKIE *comes back.*)

JACKIE   Izzy, what the fuck?

IZZY What's 337 and 362?

JACKIE 699.

IZZY That's more than two to one in favor.

JACKIE Get down from there!

IZZY I will, I will.

JACKIE Now, right now!

IZZY Don't come near me.

JACKIE Stop! I mean it!

IZZY If I fall it'll be your fault. I'm okay! Stop it!

JACKIE All right, all right. I won't touch you. Just tell me what you think you're doing.

(IZZY *is on the top level now. She begins taking off her clothes. She wears a bathing suit underneath.* JACKIE *slowly climbs toward her.*)

IZZY I know what she did wrong, you know.

JACKIE You told me that.

IZZY Too much push. She just needed to relax and let it go. That's the way it is sometimes.

JACKIE Izzy, just explain to me why you're wearing your bathing suit.

IZZY Because it looks good on me?

JACKIE Yeah, right. You're not really planning to jump, are you?

IZZY Maybe.

JACKIE You know that's crazy, right?

IZZY Maybe. That's what flying toward the sun is.

JACKIE I have no idea what you're talking about.

IZZY It's okay. Just a story.

JACKIE You need to come back down now, Iz. I mean it.

IZZY Don't come any closer, Jackie.

JACKIE I'm just talking to you. Why are you thinking about jumping, huh?

IZZY I gotta get the tape out of my head.

JACKIE What tape.

IZZY The shrink at the hospital kept talking about changing the tapes I played to myself. But it's not even tapes anymore, is it? Somebody takes out their cell and pushes a button and shit just gets recorded. It's not tape, right? It's memory? Everybody talks about how much *memory* you have. Somebody takes *their* memory and sends it to somebody else's *memory*, just like that. And everybody's *sharing memories.*

JACKIE Isabelle...

IZZY I hate the word tape. It reminds me of a tapeworm. That thing that gets inside you and eats you alive.

JACKIE You got a tapeworm?

IZZY Yeah. The one where I'm this skanky party slut.

JACKIE Come on. Let's get down from here.

IZZY I'm going to.

JACKIE Let's climb down.

IZZY No cameras. No cell phones. I'm gonna delete it. I'm gonna pull out the tapeworm.

JACKIE Do not step any closer to that...Iz!

IZZY I gotta do this, Jackie.

JACKIE Izzy, no! Could you use your brain for once in your goddamned life. Courtney couldn't do it in the daytime. It's pitch black down there.

IZZY The darkness will help, see? It'll be easy with nobody watching.

JACKIE Do not do this.

IZZY You didn't text anybody that you found me, right?

JACKIE No.

IZZY If you just take my bike out of the back of your truck, and put it back by the side of the road, then keep on driving...it will be like you weren't even here. You can erase the memory. I'm just a pain in your ass anyway.

JACKIE You think you're the only one who's ever felt like this?

IZZY I gotta pull out the tapeworm, Jackie...

JACKIE No! You're not going to pull out a fucking thing, Iz; you're not going to delete a fucking thing. If you jump, you're either going to be dead or very hurting.

IZZY I'm too sad not to do something.

JACKIE Sit down.

(JACKIE *starts to approach* IZZY.)

IZZY   Stay away!

JACKIE   Fine, I'll stay here. I'm going to sit down. You sit, too, okay?

IZZY   Why?

JACKIE   I'm going to tell you something.

IZZY   A story, like when you babysat us?

JACKIE   No, this will not be like that. This will be a story about me, okay?

IZZY   You never talk about yourself.

JACKIE   That's 'cause I don't like to.

IZZY   Why do you want to now?

JACKIE   Because I think it's something you should know, so shut up and let me talk.

IZZY   Okay.

JACKIE   You know Uncle Walter.

IZZY   I don't remember him much.

JACKIE   Yeah, well, he's in jail. He's been there for, Christ, it's been about nine years now. The family doesn't like to talk about him.

IZZY   In jail?

JACKIE   Yeah. In Missouri. They shipped him there. Anyway...

IZZY   Why's he in jail?

JACKIE   I'm getting to that, okay? You love to interrupt, you know that?

IZZY   Sorry.

JACKIE   He…liked to fool around with kids. Sexually.

IZZY   No way.

JACKIE   And put the shit online.

IZZY   No!

JACKIE   Yeah, well, before they caught him, I was…I was one of his…

IZZY   Oh, Jackie.

JACKIE   Don't. Don't "Oh, Jackie" me. I'm not telling you this so you can feel sorry for me.

IZZY   But I do.

JACKIE   Keep it to yourself, then. I'm telling you because… Isabelle, you've got to be tougher than this.

IZZY   How?

JACKIE   Stop interrupting. I thought about killing myself, too. There were pictures out there, videos worse than the shit you're in. Hell, they're still out there, I bet, on some pervert's computer. But you know what I decided? My parents put me through all that therapy shit and they were always checking in with me, but you know what finally did it for me, how I got past it?

IZZY   Uh-uh.

JACKIE   I said fuck 'em.

IZZY   Fuck 'em.

JACKIE   In my head, I said fuck Uncle Walter and fuck every pervert—fuck 'em all. I'm not talking about it any more. It's done. Finished. End of story. And whenever any thoughts come into my mind and I start to let them get to me, I just say to myself, "God damn it, they're not doing it to me again! They are not gonna fuck with my head!" And I just stopped letting 'em. Every time they come to me, I say, "Fuck you. You are not doing this to me." And I don't let 'em.

IZZY   I guess that wouldn't have made a very good bedtime story.

JACKIE   Happily ever after, not so much. The tapeworm doesn't have to play, Izzy. You're not a slut.

IZZY   Thank you for telling me, Jackie.

JACKIE   Yeah, keep it to yourself, though, okay?

IZZY   I can do that.

JACKIE   So can we go now?

IZZY   You can. I'm taking my route.

JACKIE   God damn it, Isabelle!

(JACKIE *runs and grabs* IZZY *in a hug.*)

IZZY   What are you doing?

JACKIE   I'm holding you so tight that if you go, I go.

IZZY   You're not wearing a bathing suit.

JACKIE   Doesn't matter. That's the way it's going to be, Iz.

IZZY   I'm not you. I don't know how to tell them to fuck off.

JACKIE   You just need to try. You can.

IZZY   No.

JACKIE   Say it. Tell them.

IZZY   Fuck off.

JACKIE   Yell it!

IZZY   Fuck off! Fuck off, fuck off, fuck off!

JACKIE   That's it. You don't need to spin a bottle or light a magic candle. You just need those two magic words.

IZZY   Do you like me?

JACKIE   Christ, Isabelle, no, not right at this moment. Your breath stinks and you're scarin' the shit out of me. But you're family.

IZZY   What does that mean?

JACKIE   It means… I love you. Okay?

IZZY   Thank you, Cousin Jackie.

JACKIE   You're welcome. Will you come down now? I'm tired of hanging on to you like this.

IZZY   Okay.

JACKIE   Remember the magic words, right?

IZZY   Fuck off.

JACKIE   That's right. Good. Let's go.

(JACKIE *releases* IZZY *from the full-body hug, just keeping one arm around her shoulder. She and* IZZY *cross to where they can climb down. Suddenly,* IZZY *spins away and runs to the edge of the rock.*)

JACKIE   Izzy!

IZZY   My wings won't melt. Promise.

(*She jumps.* JACKIE *runs to the rock edge, falls to the ground.*)

JACKIE   Izzy! Izzy!

◇◇

Notes on the Scene

◇◇◇◇◇◇◇◇◇◇◇◇◇◇

The third of three scenes that take place on the quarry cliff, this scene has it all: high stakes, urgency, and a set of given and emotional circumstances that the actors must bring to the scene even as it opens. There is a good deal of movement, including ongoing business that intersects with the dialogue, and physical interactions that must build with beginnings, middles, and ends. The dialogue for the most part is crisp, witty, and filled with wins, losses, and discoveries. The actors as characters must listen and react from moment to moment, even as their tactics must change in accordance with the new information that is constantly being revealed. Both characters have intricate and emotional monologues that are challenging to deliver and offer powerful storytelling opportunities for the listening actors.

In addition, the actor playing Izzy must convince Jackie and the audience that she is drunk without giving up any of her obligations to make the story clear and compelling by playing objectives, listening, and reacting. That actor must not allow herself to fall into the trap of playing drunk, but she will have great opportunities to work on her physical storytelling. In particular, several pieces of ongoing business give her the chance to create physical stories with beginnings, middles, and ends. Jackie has physical responsibilities as well. Of all the characters in the script, Jackie seems, even on the page, the most specific. Through playing objectives and making clear physical choices, the actor playing her must be able to create those particular "Jackie" characteristics. She will also have the challenge of trying to use her dominating physicality to control Izzy without endangering her in her drunken, unreliable physical condition.

The title of the scene references some wonderful metaphors found in the monologues that both reflect the characters' feeling and make statements about the meaning of the play. It will be the actors' responsibility to use those metaphors effectively, and to add to what the playwright has already provided.

CHAPTER FOURTEEN

Scene 7: Resurrections

Issues You Will Need to Consider:

Clear-cut, cause-and-effect scene

Strong, clear objectives and tactics

Discoveries, new information, wins and losses

Urgency and high stakes

Big arcs

Limited movement

Some business

Limited use of props

Listening with all senses

Wit; operatives need landing

Personal information

Lists

Monologue

COURTNEY's *room at home.* COURTNEY *is in her bed, propped up to a nearly sitting position. Her eyes are closed. A camera on a tripod faces the bed.* JACKIE *comes to the open door, knocks lightly on it, then looks into the room. Seeing* COURTNEY *asleep,* JACKIE *enters tentatively, looking around. She goes to the bureau, the desk, the computer table. At one point, she notices a prescription bottle; she picks it up, then sets it back down. As she continues to examine* COURTNEY's *room,* JACKIE's *attention keeps returning to the pills. Finally, she goes back to the bottle, picks it up again and pockets it. Her back is to* COURTNEY *when she does this.* COURTNEY *opens her eyes.*

COURTNEY   Took you long enough.

JACKIE   You're lucky I came at all. I should've just called the cops for harassment.

COURTNEY   Harassed by a cripple. Poor Jackie.

JACKIE   Cut the shit. I'm here. Your fifty-eight texts a day and your parents calling my gram every night for the past week, it all worked. I'm here. Courtney gets her way. Now what do you want?

COURTNEY   My parents saw you at the funeral.

JACKIE   Yeah, I was there.

COURTNEY   They said you spoke.

JACKIE   I'm not doing this with you. I'm not going to make small talk when we haven't even said a word to each other in the past nine years. You tell me what this is about, why you just had to have me here, and then I'm leaving.

COURTNEY   You were the last one with her. You were there when she jumped.

JACKIE   You either tell me something I don't know, or you ask whatever question you're dying to...

COURTNEY   Did she do it because of me? Did she? (JACKIE *says nothing.*) Did Izzy jump because of me?

JACKIE   Izzy jumped because she was sick in the head, and she was drunk.

COURTNEY   She didn't say anything about me?

JACKIE   What difference does it make?

COURTNEY   I think I have a right to know.

JACKIE   A right? What law, what rule are you working with that gives you a right to know anything?

COURTNEY   I think justice requires that if someone does something wrong, they should know about it.

JACKIE   So they can do what? So you can do what, Courtney? Take responsibility? Try to make things right? Justice requires? That doesn't sound like you.

COURTNEY   Did she say anything about me, Jackie?

JACKIE   No.

COURTNEY   You're lying.

JACKIE   Oh, suddenly you know me so well, we're such good friends that you can...

COURTNEY   Why are you lying to me about this?

JACKIE   Because Izzy's dead—all right?—and her parents can barely stand up they're so overwhelmed, and somehow you want to make this about you.

COURTNEY   Was it? About me?

JACKIE   Partially.

COURTNEY   Thank you.

JACKIE   For what?

COURTNEY   The truth.

JACKIE   That's not the truth. That's just one fact. Part of the truth. A small part.

COURTNEY   Then what happened?

JACKIE   Forget it. Okay. Yeah. She did it all because of you. She said, "In the name of Courtney, I am doing this. Good-bye, cruel world!" And she leapt off the cliff, screaming your name the whole fucking way down.

COURTNEY   That's okay, I don't need the details. You've told me enough.

JACKIE   I told you enough to what? I haven't told you shit.

COURTNEY   You told me enough to know that it was my fault.

JACKIE   Listen, you bitch. (*Pause*) She was up there with a candle, holding a vigil for you. She kept saying she'd studied the video and she knew what you did wrong. You pushed too hard. Somehow, in her fucked up state of mind, she thought copying

230

you, copying you but getting it right, would erase what happened to her.

COURTNEY   Thank you. I mean it.

JACKIE   Whatever. I assume this has satisfied that fucking, insatiable need you have to make everything about you. Do not text me, or bother my grandmother, any more.

COURTNEY   Okay.

(JACKIE *starts to exit.*)

Are you having a hard time sleeping?

JACKIE   What?

COURTNEY   Bad dreams?

JACKIE   I'm not playing these games...

COURTNEY   Is that why you stole my pills? To help with the nightmares? I saw you take them.

(JACKIE *comes back into the room, looks at* COURTNEY *for a second, then returns the pills to the spot she stole them from.* JACKIE *turns to exit again.*)

COURTNEY   Don't leave. Not yet. You can have the pills.

JACKIE   Fuck off.

COURTNEY   And I won't tell anyone about you trying to steal them. Your boss probably wouldn't want to hear about it, right? Sit down a minute. I have something to tell you.

(JACKIE *pauses, then comes back into the room and sits down.*)

COURTNEY   I've got this idea.

231

JACKIE   Great. The last time you let me in on one of your ideas, it didn't work out too hot. Not for me, anyway.

COURTNEY   This will.

JACKIE   Great.

COURTNEY   Look. I want you to hear me out before you say no. Okay?

JACKIE   No.

COURTNEY   I'd like to give you some money.

JACKIE   What are you talking about?

COURTNEY   I've got about fifty thousand dollars. I'd like you to have it.

JACKIE   I don't even want to respond to that.

COURTNEY   Just tell me this. What would you do if somebody just gave you fifty thousand?

JACKIE   Well, nobody's going to do that, especially you.

COURTNEY   But what would you do?

JACKIE   Look, what is this all about?

COURTNEY   What would you do?

JACKIE   I would get the hell out of this fucking town is what I would do! I would quit my job and get out of here and never come back, all right? Satisfied?

COURTNEY   How about college? Would you go to college?

JACKIE   Sure. Maybe.

COURTNEY Yeah. It was always a shame that you never did. Waste of that computer brain of yours.

JACKIE Well, that one you can take credit for, Bitch. After all that stuff came down, I just wasn't in the mood, I guess.

COURTNEY I understand. And it's another thing I can feel guilty about the rest of my life.

(*She reaches into her desk and pulls out an envelope. She throws it to* JACKIE.)

JACKIE What's that?

COURTNEY Seven thousand dollars.

JACKIE Where did this come from?

COURTNEY Here and there. I've got a crazy great-aunt who sends me five hundred every birthday and Christmas—cash and a card. Babysitting, leftovers from trips. Some I stole. I like to have a decent stash on hand that my parents can't monitor.

JACKIE Yeah, well, that's nice for you. Here.

COURTNEY No, it's yours.

JACKIE Take your fucking money.

COURTNEY It's a down payment on the fifty. The rest comes later. It's all in my account. There's a debit card in there, too, with a sticky note on it—that's the PIN number. Just in case my parents give you a hard time or something. But they won't, I promise.

JACKIE What are you talking about?

COURTNEY I'm letting you know how you'll get paid in case there's any trouble.

JACKIE   You are even crazier than everybody thinks you are.

COURTNEY   You'll take it. I don't need it. I know it can never make up for what I did to you. But it can't hurt to have it, right? A chance to start over. Where people don't know you. Don't know about you.

JACKIE   What's the catch?

COURTNEY   No catch. I know what you think of me, and believe me, it's a thousand times more positive than what I think of myself. It's just something I can do. If you let me.

JACKIE   I will never forgive you for what you did.

COURTNEY   And I don't want you to. I just want to make up for it in some small way. I told you I won't need the money.

JACKIE   Why not? Seems to me fifty grand might come in handy to someone who's gonna be pushing a wheelchair for the rest of her life.

COURTNEY   I don't plan on doing that for too long.

JACKIE   Yeah, how you gonna get around it? From what I hear, you finally bumped into something you won't be able to avoid. Or are you planning your next Super Courtney act for YouTube? Paraplegic recovers in record time. Sorry, Court. I think your luck's run out since you took that jump.

COURTNEY   I think you're right. But I also think you're gonna be wanting out of this town before too long. And that money can help make that happen.

JACKIE   What are you talking about?

COURTNEY   Oh, just what people are saying about how, if you'd been more responsible, you probably could have kept Izzy from jumping. You know, shit like that.

JACKIE   You shut the fuck up! Hear me? Shut the fuck up. I did everything I could to keep her from jumping! Everything! I held her with all my might, for god sakes. I wouldn't let go. I would never let go. Who was saying different?

COURTNEY   All you gotta do is get on Iz's Facebook page. Or Anna's, for that matter. Or just about anybody's in town. Take a look at Quarry Chat. Or Crash Landings.com.

JACKIE   It's bullshit. It's bullshit!

COURTNEY   Believe me, I know. If there's anyone, anyone, on this planet who knows how *strong*...how courageous...how *kind*...you are, it's me. Believe me, I know.

JACKIE   I hate you, all right? I fucking hate you. I did everything I could to save Izzy. I even told her about Uncle Walter. Okay? I have never talked about that day to anyone since the trial, do you understand me? But I thought if she knew...if she knew, she'd....But all me telling her did was bring back the nightmares. She jumped anyway and now, every time I try to sleep...I'm there, jumping in the water, trying to get to Izzy, going down deeper and deeper. I can't breathe. I can't see. I can't find Izzy. She isn't there. Just the blinking red light is there and I'm fucking swimming toward it. The red light from his fucking video camera and I can feel him behind me. And I know what he's doing!

COURTNEY   It's my fault. Everything.

JACKIE   Who's saying I didn't do everything I could to save her? Who's saying that? Who's saying that? Who's... (JACKIE *breaks down and begins to sob*. COURTNEY *watches*.)

COURTNEY   No one. No one is saying that. I made it up. There's nothing on Facebook, I swear. At least nothing I know about. No one is saying anything.

JACKIE   What?

COURTNEY   I said I made it up.

JACKIE   I fucking hate you.

COURTNEY   I know you do. And I deserve it. I feel the same way. So you're going to come visit me every day for the next week and a half. Okay?

JACKIE   Good luck with that.

COURTNEY   It's going to look like we've rekindled our friendship after all these years. My parents are going to be thrilled because you've helped me turn a corner and get over my depression. I'm going to convince them that they really need to get away, that it'll be good for me to have the house to myself with you for a couple of days. It won't be hard; they'll trust you by then. They'll be so grateful to you.

JACKIE   Why would I do any of this?

COURTNEY   So I can end this shit.

JACKIE   What are you talking about?

COURTNEY   You asked what's the catch that goes with the fifty thousand. That's it.

JACKIE   You said there was no catch.

COURTNEY   For you there isn't.

JACKIE   What the fuck are you talking about?

COURTNEY   I'm talking about fifty thousand dollars. A new life for you. I'm talking about you getting what you want, and me getting what I want.

JACKIE   I'm not going to...

COURTNEY   Jackie, hear me out. All you have to do is stay with me until my parents leave town. I write the note. Take care of business while you're out. And you come back and discover me. My note tells the whole story about what you did and my desire to make amends by giving you my savings. I confess about how in fear I convinced you that it would be all right for you to go with your uncle, and how I ran away and left you there and never told anyone. And how you kept my secret. All these years. I left you there by yourself, Jackie. To be molested. I didn't even try to help you. I'll never forgive myself for that. I just abandoned you, then didn't even talk to you again for nine years.

JACKIE   Yeah. That's what you did, all right.

COURTNEY   Pretty unforgivable.

JACKIE   Maybe. You know, an interesting look I see in your eyes right now—I've seen that look before.

COURTNEY   What look?

JACKIE   I don't know. Shame. Remorse. Fear. It's not a Courtney look. It's a little kid's look.

COURTNEY What are you talking about?

JACKIE Nothing. I'm just saying, it's a look I've seen before. Maybe I get it now. Maybe I always got it. Maybe that's why I never said anything. Look, I don't want your money.

COURTNEY But...

JACKIE Listen. What you did to me—leaving me there—in that basement—I think I understand. I do. Shit, Courtney, you were ten years old. You didn't even get what was going on. Not really. I knew that, I've always known that. But, see, I was always jealous of you. All these years. How you overcame all that shit. How you molded yourself into a Super Courtney. How you hid in that character and defined yourself. But I couldn't do that. I couldn't do that. I let my Uncle Walter do the defining, and I couldn't get past it.

COURTNEY Jackie...

JACKIE No, listen. The truth is I know if it happened a few years later, I know you would've acted completely differently. Cut off my uncle's balls maybe or called 9-1-1. Something. I know you would have done something.

COURTNEY That's so much more than I deserve, Jackie. I mean it. You're too much. How can you be so kind...so forgiving...so generous...? And I'm the only person in the world who knows it.

JACKIE Yeah, let's keep it that way, okay?

COURTNEY I wish I could be that generous with myself. But I can't. Besides, there's Izzy.

JACKIE Izzy? Come on, Court. Izzy always wanted to be the center of attention, but she was too fragile to handle it. Especially after the whole Internet thing.

COURTNEY Maybe. Look at me, Jackie. Look at this body. Who is this? This isn't me. I can't feel anything from my waist down. I don't even know when I'm fucking peeing on myself until I smell it. I can't walk. I can't jump. I can't dance. I can't fuck. Courtney did things. She was a rock star. People lived through me, Jackie, right? Everybody wanted to be me. Now look at me.

JACKIE People love you, Courtney. I don't know why, but they do.

COURTNEY People are sentimental fucking idiots, my parents included. You're not. I'm not. I need to take care of some business here.

JACKIE So take care of business. Kill yourself, I don't care.

COURTNEY I will; don't worry. The only problem is suicides are messy...and pitiful. I was Super Courtney. I worked hard at it. I don't want to throw it all away. I don't want the world to know how pitiful I really am. And I am pitiful. You always knew it and so did I. Now everybody will...everybody...

(COURTNEY *starts to cry.* JACKIE *looks at her for a long moment, then goes to the video camera aimed at* COURTNEY*'s bed. She turns it on.*)

JACKIE What's this here for?

COURTNEY Some stupid idea of my dad's. He thought I should post a diary on YouTube charting my progress or something. But there isn't gonna be any progress, so it's just been sitting there.

JACKIE Say hi to the world, kid.

COURTNEY What are you doing? Turn it off!

JACKIE I like your dad's idea.

239

COURTNEY   Turn that fucking thing off!

JACKIE   Here's the deal. For the next week and a half, and probably a lot longer than that, I'm coming to see you every day.

COURTNEY   Yeah, right.

JACKIE   I'm serious. I'm going to set up a blog. What should we call it? "Courtney's Return"? "The Return of Courtney"? Something like that?

COURTNEY   I am not doing this! Fuck you!

JACKIE   This is not very pretty footage so far.

COURTNEY   Go to hell, you shit! Stop it!

JACKIE   See, you painted yourself in a corner now. You've given me all this evidence about your grand plan, and if I turn it over to your parents...

COURTNEY   Don't you even...

JACKIE   Jesus, I think you'd be in for some heavy-duty therapy. And you don't wanna do therapy. Trust me on that. So, as I see it, you got two choices: Off yourself and go out as a chicken shit or...be the star of my blog. Daily video updates on Courtney's miraculous, courageous recovery.

COURTNEY   I liked you better when you were hating me.

JACKIE   Me, too. Brush your hair. You look like shit.

(JACKIE *grabs a hairbrush off the bureau and throws it to* COURTNEY.)

(COURTNEY *stares at the brush for a long moment, then picks it up and slowly starts to brush her hair.*)

JACKIE   Do you want a mirror?

COURTNEY   Go to hell.

JACKIE   Been there. Stayed far too long.

(JACKIE *gets behind the camera as* COURTNEY *continues to brush her hair. The lights fade to end the play.*)

Notes on the Scene

The actors playing Courtney and Jackie in this scene have very different challenges. As in most, if not all the scenes, the objectives are clear and the stakes are high, but this is another of those scenes with limited physical possibilities. For the actor playing Courtney, it is a matter of communicating from the waist up only. That means that all her gestures and head movements must be used to best effect. For Jackie, we must see what she is thinking and feeling through where and how she moves, and the manner in which she executes her business. Much of the scene is a verbal duel between two impassioned but extremely intelligent people. The actors must use their verbal ammunition effectively and react with great skill and imagination.

If the scene is being done in the context of the entire play, there is an incredible amount of backstory to be considered. If the scene is being done as an independent entity, the backstory invented by the actor must be thought through deeply, so that the stakes will justify the extreme actions that each character is willing to take. As soon as

Courtney opens her eyes, a life-and-death struggle begins that doesn't end until Jackie's tremendous change of heart. How and when exactly that change occurs is another of the big challenges of the scene.

There are so many dramatic moments that must be played effectively while building the clear overall arc of the scene. Some of the more important moments include the stealing of the pills, Courtney's seeing Jackie steal those pills, Courtney's demand to know whether she was responsible for Izzy's death and her response to Jackie's answer, the delivery of the proposal, the money in the envelope, Courtney's confession of wanting to end it all, the accusation that Jackie could have saved Izzy, to name a few. As for the overall arc, the journey from hate to love, from the need to punish to the need to save, from wanting to end one's life to beginning it again are all possible ways of viewing the scene, and all of these arcs are actually being traveled. Making it all clear, compelling, and believable is the challenge—but that, of course, is what good acting is.

CHAPTER FIFTEEN

Scene 8:
Cast in Stone

Open to ANNA, *recording into the voice option on her iPhone.*

ANNA   It wasn't enough. There was so much I should've said. Or
could've said. God knows, I've been thinking about it long
enough. But speaking live in front of people, to people who are
actually looking back at you, is not like talking into this. Shit!
Sorry, everybody. Sorry, Iz.

(TROY *and* ALLISON *enter, overhearing.*)

ALLISON   Hey, no—it was good.

ANNA   You weren't supposed to hear that. You were supposed to
read it. Later today, or maybe tomorrow.

TROY   Hey, what you said at the service was really nice, Anna.
Really. You said a lot of what we're all actually feeling. The tweet
is totally unnecessary.

ANNA   They all are. Do you ever feel like you're more about what you're gonna say than the something itself?

TROY   Not sure how to answer that. Let me text you on it later.

ALLISON   Ha! Funny guy.

ANNA   I don't know. The funeral was totally Mom and Dad's thing. The music, the flowers. I just wanted do something else, something she would've . . .

ALLISON   This was perfect. Outside like this. So many people came. Izzy would've loved it.

ANNA   I dunno. I hope so. Seemed so impersonal . . . just posting it on Facebook.

TROY   Can't argue with the turnout.

ANNA   Yeah, she would've loved the turnout. You're right there.

ALLISON   She would've. Definitely.

ANNA   I don't even know who half the people were.

ALLISON   Me either. At first I thought I showed up at the wrong place.

TROY   Yeah, like maybe we should have gone to the other quarry.

ALLISON   What other quarry?

TROY   It was a joke.

ANNA   Thanks, you guys. For coming, I mean. The turnout of friends, real friends. And for helping and all. For everything . . . Anyway, you know, you guys don't have to hang around.

TROY   It's no problem.

ANNA   I can't believe this is where it happened. I still can't believe it *did* happen.

ALLISON   Yeah. Maybe it's better that way, you know?

ANNA   It's just hard to imagine Izzy up there, doing that. Or maybe it's not, I don't know. But, you know what keeps popping into my head? Every time I take this place in? Even before I think of Izzy?

ALLISON   What?

ANNA   Courtney.

TROY   Whoa! I know what you mean. That girl can just dominate a room. Even outside.

ALLISON   I'm surprised she didn't come.

ANNA   I'm glad she didn't.

ALLISON   Woulda shifted the focus, huh?

ANNA   Ya think? (*A pause*) You know what this place makes me think about? When I look up at the cliff from this angle? I mean from down below?

TROY and ALLISON (*Together*)   What? (*Then*) Courtney!

ANNA   Yeah, like I said, Courtney, but it's more than that. It's what she did and why she did it. Izzy, too. What they did is connected, you know, to flying. It's like ultimate power. Think about it. Courtney sure felt it, that's pretty obvious. I know Izzy did too. Fantasies... our whole lives.

TROY   Yeah, superheroes and shit. The ones that don't fly are second stringers.

ALLISON   Am I the only one who thinks Batman sucks? Not the movies, just the concept.

ANNA   Izzy and I had a favorite story. We talked about it right before she…yeah. You know the myth about Icarus and Daedalus?

ALLISON   I had this picture book when I was a kid…

ANNA   Dulaire's?

ALLISON   Yeah! I think so.

TROY   My teacher in third grade used to read us that book before class! And show the pictures to us and shit.

ANNA   The illustrations are really great. They stay with you. At least they stayed with me. And Izzy.

TROY   Remember the picture of the one where the wax wings are melting when, which one was it, flew too high?

ANNA and ALLISON   Icarus!

ANNA   Izzy loved that myth. When she was little, though, she didn't get the flying too close to the sun part. She didn't think it was fair or something. She would never let Mom read the end of the story. She wouldn't even look at the picture of Icarus tumbling from the sky. A few years ago I like randomly picked up the book from her shelf and was leafing through it. And like on the page where Icarus is crashing, she had put x's through the feathers that had fallen off the wings and had drawn new ones to replace them.

(TROY *looks up, bothered by what he sees. He screens his eyes as he looks into the sun.*)

ALLISON What's the matter?

TROY I just thought I saw something, like on the cliff. Like a reflection off a mirror, or somethin'. There it is again.

(*They all look.*)

ANNA Somebody's up there.

ALLISON Go check it out, big boy?

TROY Naw, I...don't think so.

ALLISON Right. Thought so. He hates heights. Once was enough, right?

TROY When you do it right, once is enough.

ALLISON You're so full of it.

(JACKIE *enters.*)

JACKIE Hey, guys.

TROY Hey.

ALLISON Hi, Jackie.

JACKIE Anna, I am sooooo sorry I missed it. I don't know what to say.

ANNA It's okay. What happened? You look upset.

JACKIE I know. I am. It was crazy.

ANNA What was?

TROY Were you up on the cliff? I keep seeing a reflection. Somebody is up there.

JACKIE   It's Courtney. She's still there, I guess.

ALLISON   Courtney?

ANNA   What's she doing up there?

JACKIE   That's why I was late. I picked her up to bring her, but she insisted on going up to the top first. She wouldn't let me say no and she wouldn't tell me what for. She was getting so hysterical about it, I finally drove her up there. I had to carry her over all those rocks to the cliff. I had no idea that she was going to meet someone. And then I saw the camera... I can't believe that she got me involved. After all this. People never really fuckin' change, you know.

TROY   Tell me about it.

ALLISON   What?

TROY   Jon's up there with her, isn't he? That's a reflection off his camera I keep seeing.

ANNA   She wasn't meeting up with him, was she?

JACKIE   I had no clue, Anna. I'd never even met the kid before.

ALLISON   What are they doing up there?

TROY   I'm texting him, that moron. I'm telling him he'd better get down here...

ALLISON   How do you have his number? He still has my cell phone, that asshole. Why do you even have his number?

(TROY *says nothing.*)

ANNA   He wasn't shooting us from up there, was he? Was he recording us the whole time from up there or something?

JACKIE   I don't know what he was doing. It took me forever to get Courtney out of the car and maneuvered up the trail. The ceremony was already going by the time we got there.

ALLISON   Troy? What's the deal? Why do you have his cell phone number on your phone?

TROY   I…don't really remember how it got there.

ALLISON   You don't remember? You're fucking lying to me.

TROY   You're right, you're right. You're right. I'm sorry. Just let me send this. That fuckin' asshole should not be here.

ANNA   What's he doing up there, Jackie? Why is Courtney up there with him? What's going on? This is not right. Tell me.

JACKIE   Look, like I said. I didn't know anything about this. I guess he was interviewing Courtney up there.

ANNA   Now? During Izzy's memorial?

JACKIE   I totally agree. Once I saw what they were doing, I said forget it. That's why I left. That Jon kid can take care of her, if that's the kind of crap she's gonna pull. I'm not gonna chauffeur her around to fucking interviews.

(*We hear* TROY's *phone get a text.*)

TROY   It's Courtney. She says to wait for her. She's almost here. (*To* ALLISON) Aren't you gonna ask me why Courtney's got my number?

ALLISON   Don't be an asshole. We all know why you have her number. But you still haven't copped to why you have Jon's.

TROY   Forget about it. It's just stupid. Moving on.

ALLISON Oh, no. Too late for that now. I want to know the truth, Troy.

TROY Well, okay. It's a little complicated. When Jon and I were up on the . . .

(COURTNEY *and* JON *enter.*)

COURTNEY The truth is overrated. Believe me. If I were you guys I'd kiss and make up, instead. With tongue.

ANNA (*To* JON) You are not welcome here.

JON Hey, you never bothered to unfriend me, I figured . . .

ANNA Get the fuck out!

TROY You heard her.

JON Hey, Troy—long time, buddy.

ALLISON Long time, *buddy?*

COURTNEY Look, Anna, I'm sorry I missed the memorial. It was not my intention. I did want to pay my respects.

JACKIE You chose a strange way to do it.

COURTNEY Why does everybody have to be so pissy? Things take a little longer for me these days. I miscalculated, that's all. Come on.

ANNA Come on? Come on? You arrange for some kind of fucking interview up there, on the day of Izzy's memorial? You have this scumbag recording us without permission?

TROY Is that what you were doing?

JON Still am. It's a public place. I don't need your permission.

(TROY *goes after him again. This time* TROY *knocks* JON *down.*)

ANNA How about I don't need permission to...

JACKIE Whoa, Anna. Take it easy.

COURTNEY All right, look. This is all my fault. I'm sorry, really. I was in bad shape. Really bad shape. And I don't just mean the accident. I mean my head, all right?

JACKIE You have a magical way about you, you know?

COURTNEY Yeah, I know. Anyway, I got past feeling sorry for myself and wanting to end it all with a bottle of sleeping pills. Yeah, that's right. Super Court was going to off herself. And I would have, too.

ALLISON Courtney.

COURTNEY Oh, don't sound so shocked. Even Courtney gets the blues sometimes, especially when the doctors tell her she won't ever be able to walk again. It was a bit of a downer, you know?

ALLISON You should have told me.

COURTNEY Why would I tell *you*? You would have helped me? How, by taking odds?

TROY Hey, come on now!

ALLISON I was there for you.

COURTNEY You were there for me to keep being *me*. "Cheer up, get up, chin up. Throw your golden glow on me." I don't need that kind of shit.

JACKIE Stop it, Court!

251

COURTNEY Hey, it's the truth. Isn't that what we all want? A little truth? Well, here's some truth. Even when I became a cripple, the expectation was super comeback. That's the expectation, right? Super Court the gimp is coming back. Well that kind of shit just depressed the hell out of me, okay? I didn't have the strength. I was tired. I wanted out. And that's when Jackie got me over the hump, and I'll never forget that.

TROY I see that camera, dude. You don't want to do that.

COURTNEY Sure, he wants to do that. Let him. Get it all down, Jon—I'm on a roll! (*Moving toward* JON) You couldn't write this shit. Want me to go back and do that last part again? I'm sure I could. And I got plenty more, believe me.

ANNA Today is not about you, Courtney. You missed the memorial, so maybe you should just take it somewhere else. Have a little respect for other people. For Izzy, for god sakes. This is not about you!

COURTNEY No, no, it is, though. I woke up today and I realized: shit, I'm bored. I need to get back in the game, pick up the pace: I need to get back to the center. Find my light. And it charged me. It charged me. I went and found Jon's stuff online; I liked it...Nasty shit. I liked it. It got my heart pounding again.

JON This is going to make one hell of a documentary.

COURTNEY So...we talked. And I came to the conclusion that shooting from up there, right from the scene of the crime, or crimes, whatever, with Izzy's ceremony going on down here, would be a fitting way for me to start getting my fucking life back.

ANNA Oh, my god! That is such bullshit. Nasty selfish bullshit.

COURTNEY Oh, fuck you, Anna! Fuck you all! You know, I did have one funny thought while I was up there. Just for a second, I had this little impulse to just tip my wheelchair over and fly right off the rock. Would have felt really good, too. Really good. Going out flying, Yeah! That would have made a good shot, huh, Jon?

JON Pretty dramatic, all right.

COURTNEY And ironic. An ironic and tragic ending for your documentary. I'd say much award-winning potential.

JON I don't know. I'd want multiple angles. And lots of quick cuts in the edit.

COURTNEY Really? I would think the shot of me going over the edge in slo-mo maybe: "Good-bye, cruel world!" Then, of course, you could get my crumpled body from above.

ANNA Stop it. Stop it! This is so fucking sick.

ALLISON Anna, she's been drinking.

COURTNEY Oh, you picked that right up this time, huh? She is capable of learning, ladies and gentlemen. Have you learned anything about betting on the odds, bitch? About handicapping? No pun intended. Remember to check out the wind factor before making any stiff bets?

ALLISON Hey, what are you...

COURTNEY Yeah, bitch, I found out about that!

ANNA I don't care if you're drunk. I don't care if you're in a wheelchair.

JON   Watch it. Don't let Anna get too pissed off. She can get violent.

ANNA   You have nothing to say here, asshole!

TROY   Yeah, shut up, asshole.

JON   You two going out now? How did you happen to seal the deal on that?

TROY   Shut the fuck up!

ALLISON   What is he talking about? Troy?

ANNA   How dare you come here like this? Talk about getting your life back? This was supposed to be about Izzy. Not you. Not everything is about you. You have no right!

JACKIE   Anna, take it down a notch. We can talk it through.

COURTNEY   No, no, let her have her say. She's right. I deserve it.

ANNA   You come here on Izzy's memorial and have the fucking nerve to bring this low-rent Little League journalist so you can work on getting your goddamned life back? How about my sister's life? Are you going to do anything about that, or have you completely forgotten that you were the one that killed her! She was copying you, Courtney! She did this because she wanted to be like you!

COURTNEY   That's ridiculous. She didn't want to be like me. She just wanted some of the attention I get. That's all. She was too weak to be me. I know that. So do you.

ANNA   Don't you dare talk about her. You didn't know her.

COURTNEY   I knew her enough to see she had a good heart, the kind that gets broken easily. The wrong kind of heart for fifteen fucking minutes of fame. Simply the facts, Anna. Did you get that, Jon?

JON Oh, yeah. I got it all. Good stuff.

COURTNEY You're the man.

JON Don't I know it.

COURTNEY Let's get out of here. Mission accomplished. (JON *starts to wheel* COURTNEY *away. She speaks to* ANNA.) Hey, I am sorry. I may be a little drunk, but I am really sorry. Truly.

(JON *and* COURTNEY *exit. They all watch.* TROY *moves to take* ALLISON's *hand, but she pulls away from him and exits.* TROY *looks toward* COURTNEY *for a moment and then runs to catch up with* ALLISON. ANNA *turns to look up at the rocks above.* JACKIE *moves to* ANNA *and embraces her for a few moments.* JACKIE *leaves.* ANNA *turns out and begins to speak into her phone.*)

ANNA So what I was really trying to say is that when I saw all those faces out there in front of me, I got nervous, and decided to throw away this little speech I had actually sat down and written. (*She rummages for the speech and unfolds it.*) I thought it was a little too pat or something. A little too honest, maybe. But now in hindsight, I think I should have just read it. Anyway, here's the important part. (*She finds the part she wants and reads.*) "Icarus and Daedalus was always Izzy's favorite Greek myth, so I can't help making a connection between the story and how she died. But here's the thing: Izzy never really understood the story. She just thought it was unfair that Icarus died. She never got that Icarus died because he was doing something he loved doing. Not to escape his island prison, not because it would make him famous, or make him feel good about himself. (*The lights start to* *fade.*) Not because he wanted to set a new record for height or distance...not for his fifteen minutes, not because he wanted people to like him or something...he just did it because...because...he wanted to FLY!"

End of Play

◇◇

It would go beyond the scope of this book to take apart the scene above. Unlike the other scenes in this play, intentionally structured between two characters so the conflict could be more easily recognized and developed, this multi-character scene automatically becomes far more complex. Let me just throw out a hint or two. There are several two-person conflicts going on in this scene, of course, but there are also larger conflicts in which the characters take sides. There will also be questions about the center of focus; that is, whose story should the audience be primarily following at any particular time in the scene? It will be your job as an actor to know when you are the center of action and when you are not. It will be your responsibility to make choices that are clear, compelling, and believable throughout. But it will also be your responsibility to do so in a way that throws focus where it should be throughout the scene so that the story is always clear and compelling. If you do take on this scene in a classwork situation, it will probably require an outside eye to help you get the arc and clarity just right. In this kind of acting situation, even when you're director proof, you may still need that director!

Break a leg.

AFTERWORD

I have been teaching acting as a full-time occupation for over twenty-five years, and I didn't always teach the way I do now. I have changed and evolved as a teacher in accordance with what I think students need and how I can best serve the class I am currently teaching. When I began, I was always running to and from the stage area to demonstrate a point that would instantly solve a problem. There was always a physical action I could inflate for a laugh while making a teaching moment. But my teaching technique was heavily reliant on "Do it like this." And when my students copied me (sans the exaggeration), they would feel successful—for the moment. I realized after a while, though, that showing my students what to do did not necessarily give them the skills to solve the next acting problem they would face or better enable them to work independently. I was going for the product of a moment rather than teaching a way of thinking about acting. Today, it is unusual for me to enter the stage area during class. When I do it often means that I have exhausted my arsenal of verbal approaches.

Although my teaching has always been action-based, my focus has continued to change to meet the needs of today's students. I have observed that in general the student actors I work with today tend to see things more in black-and-white than my students from years ago. Things are either this way or that way. They want the right answer to solve a problem and they want it immediately. Shades of gray and ambiguity frustrate them. They have fewer social skills in dealing with their fellow acting students than in years gone by, and fewer insights as to what makes people behave as they do. As developing artists, they are far less comfortable hearing criticism than students were years ago, and less accustomed to pursuing long-term goals rather than immediate gratification. They are also much more uncomfortable with their physical selves and rely much more on their words than on their physicality in their interactions. Maybe some or all of this sounds familiar to you?

I understand that many if not all of the characteristics I have just described probably also reflect our society at large, and so be it. I could go into a long treatise on my theories of why this is so, but it doesn't really matter for our purposes here. The problem is that the characteristics I have described above all work against you as an actor. The analysis process that we explored in the first section of the book assumes that you have an understanding of people and how they behave. It assumes that you have absorbed through observation and study what motivates people and what they will do and how they might do it under particular conditions. It assumes that your own life experiences have been deep enough and varied enough to give you a body of information about how human beings behave that you can draw from before making your acting choices. But these assumptions are not necessarily true.

As a teacher, I too have had to absorb my observations about people—most importantly, students—into my work. I spend a lot more time with analysis than I used to do. Students must think about why characters behave as they do before they can make choices about what those characters should be doing. And I spend much more time developing my students' listening skills. If people don't listen to each other accurately and carefully in life, how are they going to be able to do it better as actors when there are so many other things to be thinking about? I also spend much more time focusing on physical acting—telling the story with the body as well as the words, moving from place to place believably and with purpose, using props realistically and effectively, touching other characters with clarity and emotional truth, etc.

I have adjusted my teaching because what is important to me is turning my students into good actors regardless of what they bring to the table. I am still always looking for the best ways to make my actors independent and director proof. That means I want my students to be able to produce good acting—acting that is believable, and tells the best possible story while serving the script—completely on their own. Remember, in the profession, once you have been hired, the director assumes you are a good actor and is not too concerned with trying to make you look like one. Directors expect you to bring the gold independently. If you don't produce what they need, you will be replaced. It is that simple. Therefore you must be able to do your work without having someone tell you how to do it.

The biggest change in my teaching has been in the amount of time I spend on script analysis. I hope you have a good understanding now of why analysis is an essential part of your craft. You can't do your job well if you don't know what your job is. Your job is telling the story effectively, and you simply can't do that without being able to recognize what the story is and how it works. That means analysis. But once you know what the story is and how it works, it becomes your job to tell the story through what you do. That means making choices that are believable and that tell the story with all the clarity and excitement you can bring to it. Then, when you have synthesized those choices into a performance through practicing and working with others, you need to be able to tell that story on stage while listening and reacting in the moment. Ultimately, you must be able to do all of these things reliably if you are going to be a successful actor.

As I close out the current fall semester, I am writing final evaluations for students in an introduction to acting craft (for freshmen), a sophomore scene study class, and an advanced acting class for seniors. What is most interesting to me is the fact that despite their differences in experience and ability, the problems that each group encountered in their finals preparation all stemmed from the challenge of analyzing that material effectively, making choices that clarified and enhanced that story, and, ultimately, their ability to listen and react in the moment.

My freshman class spent the semester focusing on how to use the basic tools of acting that they had been introduced to. The final gave them their first opportunity to apply those tools to a complete scene with dialogue. Previously, the froshies had done their prepared acting work only through exercises, etudes, and short scenes with no given context. The final was their only opportunity to put it all together. The sophomores spent the semester working on scenes from contemporary plays that were realistic in style. They were required to approach their scenes in the context of the entire play. All dialogue in their selected scenes was simple and direct. In other words, the characters the sophomores took on sounded pretty much like people do in real life. In contrast, the seniors spent the semester working with nineteenth-century European plays—Chekhov, Ibsen, and Strindberg. These, by necessity, were all translated works. The Ibsen interpretations tended to be formalized and wordy, making it difficult for the actors to sound off-the-cuff and believable. In Chekhov, on the other hand (translated by first-rate English and American playwrights), the stories hid themselves cleverly in the subtext beneath the spare and seemingly empty dialogue.

For the freshmen, working on actual scenes from plays proved to be a challenge. At semester's end, many of them still struggled to find and tell the story of a script independently, clearly, and compellingly.

Listening and reacting believably in the moment while meeting these other obligations was, to put it simply, too many balls to juggle. It may sound surprising that so many of the students were challenged even to identify and articulate the story, given that stories are a part of our lives from the time we can listen, and—more to the point—one of the founding principles of the semester. However, the difference between being able to listen to a story and being able to articulate it effectively is vast. As many of you have discovered while working with the contents of this book, understanding the concepts and being able to apply them effectively are very different things, and proficiency requires far more repetition and practice than any single semester can provide.

Despite knowing what they *should* do in approaching the material, many of my froshies defaulted back to their high school habits. They forgot, for instance, to start with the conflict and objectives present in their scenes. Many found it difficult to simply express an objective even when they claimed to know what it was. Almost all of the freshmen, even those who found an objective to play, were unable to pursue that objective and stay with it as they moved through their cutting. Those who could still had difficulty finding or maintaining the urgency and stakes in those scenes. Several who focused on urgency lost believability by pushing too hard or emoting falsely. In short, only a few froshies were able to stay on the railroad track the playwright had provided—at least, on their own. Encouragingly, all of the scenes eventually improved when notes and suggestions were given. In fact, by the time the rest of the acting faculty observed the work, the scenes were fairly impressive. The trick, however, and the ultimate goal, as you have been reading in this book, is to be able to do all of this work independently.

The sophomores also found it difficult to identify and tell the story clearly on the first put-up of the final scene they would present.

However, their ability to make adjustments after those first put-ups demonstrated how much they had grown in a single year. (The ability to make adjustments quickly and efficiently is a strong marker for weighing the development of craft, but should not be confused with being able to work with complete independence, your ultimate goal.) When the sophomores failed to tell the story clearly, it was often a result of missing important information from the given circumstances or a failure to understand what the characters really wanted from each other. Unlike the freshmen, they rarely missed the story completely.

Sometimes, the sophomore scenes didn't work because the actors failed to recognize and make choices based on the genre of their selected plays. A comedy, for instance, played as a drama can make for a very strange scene. Actors must be able to recognize when characters are using their wits to get what they want. And they must land the jokes and witticisms those characters come up with clearly and effectively. Otherwise, the characters will not be believable, and neither will the story.

Yet the sophomores had worked hard during the semester to find and maintain believable behavior on stage—to sound and move like real people do. Most of them had discovered how to sound real by making everything they said conversational. Each of them had developed personal acting tricks to make it sound like they weren't acting. But when they first put up their final scenes, the dramatic arc built in by the playwright was invariably missing. As the students worked to coordinate the realistic behavior they had worked so hard on with their obligation to the story, urgency and high stakes fell by the wayside. And low stakes and a lack of urgency seldom make for an exciting play.

With notes in hand and further rehearsal, most managed to up the stakes considerably, and by the time the faculty saw the work, the scenes were vastly improved. Yet in order to be truly compelling, the students would need to become practiced at the seemingly spontaneous moment-to-moment work that follows skillful analysis and choices. Some were already demonstrating good listening and reacting in the moment, but learning to master this combination of skills is not a short-term operation.

Meanwhile, many of the sophomores had had their first performance experiences during the semester (BFA freshman actors are not permitted to act in productions in many programs, including ours). Several were cast in a musical whose director gave actors a lot of freedom, expecting each one to bring his own choices to the rehearsal. Some of the actors, left to their own devices, were frustrated, and some floundered. More than one made choices that prevented the audience from liking them, and their performances were not successful. They weren't yet proficient at making choices consistent with the world of the play—in this case, a world of charm and romance.

If this was a challenge for these beginning actors, it paled compared to what awaited them in their senior year. For their final, the seniors had to remount some of their best work of the semester. They began their course work with scenes from Chekhov—whose characters, in his major plays, essentially don't know what they want or how to get it. They suffer from an inability to genuinely know their own hearts and minds. They are used to being taken care of, and don't know how to operate in a new world where they must learn to make their own way. This is the Russia of the late nineteenth century, where the out-of-date social system is being upended. For our purposes here, you don't need to know the historical and sociological hows and whys, but actors doing these scenes certainly must. In order to understand their characters, the seniors had to educate themselves about the world in which their characters lived. This kind of background research did not come into play for the sophomores and freshmen, but it is essential to making good choices when doing plays that are not contemporary.

Without this kind of understanding, making choices for a Chekhovian character would be even more difficult than it already is.

But even when an actor understands the world that Anton Chekhov wrote about, the task remains difficult because Chekhovian characters operate in a way that makes applying action-based acting very challenging. How, for instance, can an actor find his character's objective when the character seems to have none; when a character seems to do almost nothing during the course of the play? And how, when characters don't really know themselves or what they really want and need, can the actors playing them find the clues in the dialogue for telling the story of the play and its characters? And since there is so little action, what is that story that has to be told, or there is one at all?

It is true that very little of consequence seems to happen during the course of a major Chekhov play, but that means that what little does happen must be considered as extremely important. The clues to the characters' objectives, their wants and needs, are in the script—even when the characters themselves don't know what they are—but with Chekhov, actors must work harder to find them. Once they do, they must turn those clues into choices and those choices into actions—actions they will play with the greatest amount of believable urgency possible. Without making choices for their characters—choices that serve and enhance the play—the primary obligation to serve the story becomes impossible.

Since the dialogue from moment to moment does not necessarily offer significant clues to a Chekhovian character's heart and mind, or, for that matter, to his or her often subconscious objectives, an actor must pay very close attention to the character's arc in the entire play, and to the details in the overall story. Particular attention must be paid to the arc of interrelationships of characters throughout the course of the play. Subtle references to people, places, and things must be noted and studied. At times, certainly for actors unfamiliar with his works, it may be necessary to find criticism and reviews on Chekhov's plays before setting out to make their own choices. This is not cheating; this is necessary research, and it is part of the analysis that every actor must engage in.

So, for the seniors, finding the story, buried and seemingly invisible, was the first and most significant obligation they had to tackle. No different from the task that the sophs and froshies faced—just far more challenging in a play by the good Dr. C.

The plays by Ibsen and Strindberg presented yet another kind of problem, but still rooted in finding and telling the story effectively. Though Ibsen's dialogue, in translation at any rate, seems prosaic and endless, the actor must find a way to cut through the verbiage and give the audience a compelling story—the one the playwright intended. That means finding the big moments of discovery, loss, and victory, and playing them with great clarity. It means creating characters through physical and psychological actions that are compelling and capable of moving us. Particular attention must be paid to how the big moments move the plot forward and make clear the arc of the scene and character. What the actor chooses to do physically as the character—in terms of movement, gesture, and ongoing business—becomes critically important to making the action clear and to understanding a character's inner life. If the actor relies on the dialogue alone to advance the story, he is sentencing the audience to a long and dull evening of theatre. The story is there, the characters have plenty to do, but it is the actor who must find the way to deliver both action and character with clarity.

It becomes particularly important to consider how the audience should perceive these characters, and that starts with their function in the play's machinery. In other words, how must the audience respond to these characters in order for the action of the story and character to work effectively? Once that is determined, the actor must figure out the choices that will create the appropriate responses to his character. This cannot be left to accident.

Besides the basic difficulty of cutting through the dialogue and finding the action contained therein, the seniors found it challenging to invent physical action to support that dialogue and clarify it. When to move, where to move, and what to do were ongoing challenges to believability and clarity of story. Coming up with ongoing business that could help shape the big moments and reveal character became an essential part of the actors' focus. But ultimately, what they learned in terms of shaping business and movement made the Ibsen work a favorite for most of the seniors.

Of particular note was the fact that many of the seniors, because of the stodginess of the dialogue, at first perceived the Ibsen and Strindberg characters as far less dimensional than they actually are. They saw most of the characters as good guys or bad guys, and as a result tended to make black-and-white, simplistic choices in portraying them. Hedda was a moustache twirler because she manipulated the characters who shared the scene with her. Nora was either a simpleton, if an early scene was chosen, or purely evil, if a later scene was chosen. How could she be anything else if she could make the choice to abandon her children? Krogstad was a bad guy because he tried to blackmail Nora, etc. In every case, the seniors initially forgot that—creaky dialogue notwithstanding—these plays are in the style of realism and the characters are complex (meaning that they have many levels and contradictions). On a more basic level, the seniors forgot to ask themselves how the audience must perceive their characters if the over-all play was to work effectively. And, of course, once again, with a bit of coaching, the class quickly made the necessary adjustments. The scenes and their work in those scenes improved—quickly and significantly.

When the seniors remounted their selected work for the final, the scenes were stronger still. Because of the preliminary work they had already done and the rehearsal process they had already gone through, they could bring the scenes quickly up to speed. This allowed the actors to spend most of their time working on the scenes organically. They already knew the scenes in terms of preparation and in terms of choices. The scenes were already in their muscle memories. That enabled the actors to focus almost exclusively on the third part of the acting trinity: staying in the moment and listening and reacting. Their scenes were very impressive indeed, filled with interesting and seemingly spontaneous moments! What more could an audience or acting teacher ask for?

So that brings me to the end of our journey together. One last thought before you close this book and return it to the shelf. *Acting on the Script* has been all about developing craft—a skill set that must be mastered—and I have said that mastery takes time. In many recent books, including best sellers such as *Outliers* by Malcolm Gladwell, the ten-thousand-hour rule has been cited. To summarize, the ten-thousand-hour rule states that any skill of note takes at least that amount of time—ten thousand hours—to master. Analysis and synthesis are those kinds of skills, and it is likely to take you a long time to truly master them. I am fairly good at these skills at this point in my teaching career. Why shouldn't I be? I have been doing this kind of work with dedication for thirty years or so. That should have given me more than the requisite number of hours. But I still remember my first acting class, and I still remember my first year of graduate school. And I still remember my first year of teaching, when, time and again, I could not explain to my students why I thought what I thought about a particular scene or moment. I put in the hours, and now I have the skills.

I am no smarter than you are. But I have logged the hours. You'll get there, too. Just do the work, and continue to enjoy the journey.

ACKNOWLEDGMENTS

I didn't really understand the craft of acting until I had to teach it. Unlike actors who can fake their way through by using their talents, instincts, and experience, teachers actually have to be able to explain the craft they are doling out. And if what they are explaining fails to make sense or seems too complicated, student actors will give up on it quickly. And it was only when I learned how to articulate craft—simply and clearly—so that it did make sense, that my students really started making great leaps toward mastery. I have learned from every one of them, and I thank them all.

It was no different when I started writing about acting craft, except that my words had to be even more precise and even more carefully chosen. And like learning craft, learning to write about it took a lot of time and a lot of help. For that reason, I would like to send out special thanks to Don Corathers and Jim Palmarini, my editors at *Dramatics* magazine and *Teaching Theatre* journal, respectively, who kept me writing and gave me the opportunity to learn how to do it. I will always be grateful for their guidance and encouragement, and for the opportunities they gave me.

I would also like to express my appreciation to all those who helped make this book possible and as good as it could be—my editorial team at Hal Leonard Performing Arts Publishing Group, especially Marybeth Keating whose low key grace and wisdom made this and all my books for Hal Leonard a pleasure to work on.